THE BIG BO OF "WHY" FOR PARENTS

75 TIPS AND TRICKS FOR NEW PARENTS

CLIFFORD DALE JAMES III,
BS, MD, FAAP

Skyhorse Publishing

Skyhorse Publishing books may be purchased in bulk at special discounts for sales promotion, corporate gifts, fund-raising, or educational purposes. Special editions can also be created to specifications. For details, contact the Special Sales Department, Skyhorse Publishing, 307 West 36th Street, 11th Floor, New York, NY 10018 or info@skyhorsepublishing.com.

Skyhorse® and Skyhorse Publishing® are registered trademarks of Skyhorse Publishing, Inc.®, a Delaware corporation.

Visit our website at www.skyhorsepublishing.com.

10 9 8 7 6 5 4 3 2 1

Library of Congress Cataloging-in-Publication Data is available on file.

Cover design by Mona Lin
Cover photo credit: iStockphoto

ISBN: 978-1-5107-5816-2
Ebook ISBN: 978-1-5107-5817-9

Printed in China

Dedication

This book is dedicated to the memory of my dad, Clifford Dale James, Jr. He always instilled in me the need to question "Why." After all these years, I'm still asking "Why?" and through this book, I'm answering somebody else's "Why" questions as well.

Disclaimer

Although this book is written by a medical professional, it is not in any way meant to replace your child's actual doctor. Information in this book is meant to educate, entertain, and ease some worry, but is in no way meant to diagnose any medical condition or prescribe treatment. We do not assume any liability for medical decisions that you make on your own without the aid of a medical professional who actually cares for your child.

Acknowledgments

I would like to recognize William Nave and thank him. Trust me, you should thank him as well. My wife has often commented that I never met a comma I liked. Bill was responsible for turning my words into actual sentences that could be read and understood. He was able to take pages of run-on sentences and turn them into actual paragraphs and something that could be read by actual people. You will also occasionally see a cooking reference show up in this book. I am a terrible cook, but Bill is an amazing chef and liked to "spice" things up every once in a bit with a cooking reference. He was able to actually spell, punctuate, and know how to use a thesaurus, so this book could actually exist. Again, thank you Bill for helping me make this book happen.

I would also like to thank my wife, Kristi, and my children Dalton, Tyler, and Kaden. They have come up with some of their own questions and made me ask a few of my own. They have had to give up a lot having a pediatrician in the house, and I'm thankful they put up with me while I do the job I love.

I would like to thank my staff: Amanda Moore, Ashley Runkles, Brittany Bishop, Kesha Dryman, Shelbie Faulkner, Melissa Maupin, Mel Sisco, and Tonya Thomas. They help me get all the stuff done on a daily basis so I have time to write this book. Thank you for making me look a lot better than I would on my own.

Finally, I'd like to thank all my patients. Over the years, you have given me the joy and pleasure of answering each and every one of these questions. I am so thankful for getting the chance to answer the questions and be a part of each of your families.

Table of Contents

Introduction

Welcome to *The Big Book of "Why" for Parents*!

This book is intended to answer the questions that as a pediatrician I hear the most often that start with "WHY."

You will notice that I have tried to divide up the book into some time spans within a baby's first couple of years so you can jump around and reference the questions (and answers!) most easily. Nevertheless, it's true that not everyone asks a particular question at the same point in time and also the fact that every baby is different and hits certain milestones at different times so they can prove authors like me wrong.

This book is by no means all-inclusive to all the "WHY's" you could possibly come up with; it just covers the most common.

You will notice some glaring deficiencies! We don't really cover how to diagnose anything or how to treat things. The reason is that this book cannot replace your baby's pediatrician. If your baby is blue, having problems breathing, not growing, having a high fever . . . you need to call your doctor. Don't be consulting this book or browsing the Internet to try and be the doctor. Your baby is too precious for you to wait the required 11 years to be well trained in pediatrics in order for you to trust your diagnosis skills. If you can't trust your pediatrician to help you when you are worried about your baby, then it is time to find a new pediatrician.

This book is meant to be an easy read. I have tried to make it informative, make you feel better about some of the unknowns, and even make you smile from time to time. Enjoy your time being a parent! It goes by extremely slowly in the beginning, but seems to disappear in the blink of an eye. Try to consciously slow time down and live in the now.

Enjoy each one of the WHY's that your child's life has to offer.

PART 1

BEFORE THE BABY
IS BORN

"A baby is something you carry inside you for nine months, in your arms for three years, and in your heart until the day you die."

—*Mary Mason*

Istock.com/Blue Planet Studio

Why do I need to choose a doctor before my baby is born?

Seems like a weird idea, right? I have to choose a doctor for a baby that I haven't even met yet? The answer is an absolute *yes* for all kinds of reasons.

Let's just come out and say it—not all doctors are created equal. There are good doctors, great doctors, average doctors, and even bad doctors. You will want to find out who the good ones are before you ever have your baby.

But how do you find the good doctors? This gets a little tougher.

First, I would recommend going online and looking at how they are rated on different websites that grade physicians. Make sure that you read the reviews strategically. You generally are looking for the great ones and the terrible ones. Some of the terrible ones could be legitimate cause to pass on a practice. The glowing 5-star reviews deserve a little scrutiny too. If 10 different "patients" all gave a glowing review in a short time period, used similar language, and no other reviews seem to correlate . . . well . . . just look closely, okay? The Internet is a weird place. Be careful out there.

Let me give you a personal example. I have a one-star review from someone I haven't even met. She is an activist from California who was attacking me because my first book didn't come out against circumcision. She was going on and on about how inhumane I was and a terrible doctor. I have never done

Istock.com/Michael Jung

a circumcision. I have never even seen one done. I told her off and she gave me a one-star review. The website refuses to remove it so I am stuck with a review from someone who has never even met me. So, if you see a doctor who has a bunch of glowing reviews and a couple of bad ones, they are likely a good choice. Don't throw them out just because of upset, crazy people. Like I said—Internet. Weird, very weird.

Second, ask your friends and neighbors. There is a good chance that the people you hang out with will share some of your same values and beliefs. They will also know your personality and how you will fit in to certain offices and with different physicians. I will tell you that most people you talk with will have limited experience in this realm. If they like their doctor, they may have only seen one doctor. It is hard to compare who is best when you have only seen one or two.

The last way I would explore options is to ask your OB/Gyn or the hospital where you are delivering. This may provide the most accurate overall assessment. They tend to know the different doctors better and all the options out there. They don't have anything personal in the selection and can likely give the best advice on a physician's reputation in the community.

Once you have gone through the investigation phase, now it is time to start narrowing down the list. I recommend you narrow down the list to two or three practices that you have some recommendations for so it doesn't seem overwhelming.

There are a few practical things that you should look into about each of the offices that

you have on your list. First, do they take your insurance? This can be found out on your insurance's website, from your insurance agent, or just by calling each of the practices and asking.

Second, are their hours of operation going to work around your hours? Doctors will vary their hours to fit their lives or to offer something different to their patients. I have seen offices that are open on bankers' hours, I have seen offices with really long hours, and I have seen offices that are only open in the afternoon and evening. Make sure the hours they are open work for you and your schedule. Think ahead to going back to work and to when your child is in school. Find out about weekend and holiday hours as well. They might be a fantastic doctor, but if your life conflicts with their schedule in a way that makes it difficult for you to see them, that's a deal breaker.

The last pragmatic question is a biggie— are they taking new patients? It would be terrible if you got your heart set on a specific practice only to find out they won't even take your new baby.

Now comes the fun part. Go see the office and meet the doctor. This visit is important for all kinds of reasons. One—this gives you a chance to interact with the front office as you make the appointment and then come into the office. Are they nice, do they answer the phone, are they helpful, do they smile? Check out the office. Is it clean? Is there some way to entertain a little one while you are waiting for the doctor? Do you like the way it looks? Now go talk to the doctor. Do they seem nice? Do they answer your questions? Do they seem in a hurry? Do they fit your personality?

When I have expectant parents come and talk to me, I always try to tell them the same thing: The most important part of finding a pediatrician is, do you feel comfortable talking to them? Most of the time we pediatricians find out what is wrong with your baby by the story. We listen closely when you are asking us "what is wrong with my baby?" Most of the time you are telling us what is wrong at the same time you are asking the question. We are examining your baby to make sure that what we learned from the story is correct, but most of the time the key is in the story. If you don't feel comfortable talking to us, then you won't give us the whole story and your child's care will suffer. Just like regular people, doctors come with all kinds of personalities. Some personalities will get along with you better than others. Make sure your pediatrician fits in with you and your family.

Once you have narrowed down your search to your chosen pediatrician and pediatric office, then it is time to get ready for introducing the baby. Make sure you know what you will need as far as paperwork before that first visit. Ask when you will need to see them first. Some pediatricians will see you in the hospital, and some will see you when the baby is 3 to 5 days old. It is just nice to know what to expect in the chaos that is soon going to happen.

This is a very important decision for you and your family. Your pediatrician will be invaluable in guiding you down the path of raising a happy, healthy child. Take some time and set yourself up for success with the right practice and the right doctor.

TAKE-HOME POINTS:

1. Find out the pediatrician's reputation online, with your friends, and with the medical professionals.
2. Find out if the practice takes your insurance and if the days and hours of operation work with your schedule.
3. Go visit the practice so you can make the most informed decision about your baby's caregiver.
4. Ask them questions that are important to you as a family; don't just depend on the questions that you can find on the Internet.

Why is breast milk best?

This is a bit of a loaded question. Breast milk is best because it was what babies were meant to eat. Science is great and all, but mom's natural milk cannot be topped by a lab. Mother Nature made it just for babies, and it is wonderful stuff. Even scientists who are always trying to convince us they can do it better have had to agree that study after study has proven that breast milk beats all the man-made formulas we have come up with over the years.

That said, formula does still have a place. I have been a pediatrician long enough to know that formula has absolutely saved some babies' lives. Formula is incredibly useful and very healthy for babies. Yet if we are comparing head to head between breast milk and formula, breast milk wins every time.

But why?

Let's start off with bonding. There is something special for a mom to be able to make milk that contains everything that her baby needs to grow and thrive. When everything works the way it is supposed to, breastfeeding your baby is very empowering. It's a girl power, superhero kind of thing. When you are a breastfeeding mom you are the one who can fix it, you can conquer the evil of hunger single-handedly. Being the sole source of food can offer a great bonding experience all on its own. Now add in the warmth, the snuggling, and the closeness that the two of you will share multiple times a day. Trust me, at some point Dad is going to get jealous of the special bond you have with your breastfeeding baby. It will not be happening at the 2 a.m. feeding, but it will happen.

Next, let's talk about taste and temperature. Evidently, baby taste buds were made to love the taste of breast milk. Trying to get a breastfed baby to take anything else can sometimes be quite the chore. It has the perfect amount of everything and tastes like exactly what they want. Plus, when it is coming straight from mom, it's at the perfect temperature. You can't duplicate that with a bottle, no matter how hard you try. If a baby takes a break in feeding, when they come back the breast milk is still the perfect temperature. It is always fresh too.

Okay, so we have covered bonding, taste, temperature, and freshness. What happens next, after they have consumed the milk? Yep. Breast milk wins again. I don't think there is a pediatrician on the planet who will argue formula is easier to digest. Babies eating breast milk have less problems with gas or bellyaches and are very rarely constipated. It's kind of like they were made to eat the stuff. An extra little bonus is that breastfed babies have better smelling poop. Don't get me wrong—it still smells like poop, just not as stinky.

The benefits don't stop there. As long as you don't calculate the time it takes to breastfeed (which, to be honest, the time commitment is going to be great no matter what type of milk you feed your baby), breast milk is free. Mom is going to be hungrier than normal for sure, so I guess there's a small cost there. When you compare Mom eating bigger portions to the cost of bottles, formula, bottle liners, dish soap to clean everything, gas for the car to buy all this stuff ... well, you get the idea. Plus, you don't have to run to the store at 3 a.m. with a screaming, hungry baby to buy more breast milk. So, there's that.

Convenience is also one of the categories that breastfeeding can win, with a little caveat. Breast milk is always with you as the mom. This can present an issue if the baby is not with Mom. Pumping breast milk is definitely not convenient, but given all the other benefits it's a small price to pay.

I saved the best for last. Let's talk about health. It would be impossible to say that your baby would be healthier drinking formula than breast milk. Long-term studies have shown that babies who breastfeed have fewer vomiting and diarrhea illnesses, fewer issues with constipation and gas, and fewer

problems with obesity. There are other studies underway that are trying to demonstrate breastfed babies' improvement in intelligence and overall health as well.

It is pretty easy to argue that breast milk is the best for your baby, but it isn't always possible for moms to breastfeed. There are moms who physically can't produce breast milk for many different reasons. There are medical conditions in babies that force them to drink specialty formula. There are situations in life that make it difficult for a mom to be able to breastfeed. I don't think you should feel guilty as a mom if you choose to not breastfeed. I think most of us as parents are trying to do the best we can to take care of our families. We're all just trying to give them the best start in life we know how to do.

TAKE-HOME POINTS:

1. Your baby was made to eat breast milk.
2. Breastfeeding is a great way to bond with your baby.
3. Your baby has taste buds that appreciate the taste of breast milk.
4. Breast milk is FREE.
5. Your baby will probably be healthier eating breast milk.
6. The best thing for your baby is to feed them. If breast milk is not a possibility, do not grade your value as a parent on the type of milk your baby drinks.
7. We in the baby profession all know that breastfeeding is hard and comes with sacrifices. If you have breastfed your baby or even tried to breastfeed your baby, give yourself a pat on the back. You deserve it!

Why are there different types of formula?

I think the best place to start when talking about formula is at the beginning. There have always been babies who couldn't eat breast milk. The reasons for this are varied. Sometimes Mom had to stay late at work because *some people* don't grasp the concept of deadlines. Sometimes Mom is not able to produce breast milk. Sometimes the baby is not able to eat from the breast. Some babies have an intolerance to mother's milk. Tragically, mothers died in childbirth in years past, in far greater numbers than they do

Istock.com/miodrag ignjatovic

today. All of these situations involve an infant who needs nutrition, and breast milk isn't an option.

Historically, many steps were taken to try to solve this problem. There were wet nurses who could be paid to breastfeed a baby that was not their own. Then there were animal milks, such as cow or goat milk most commonly. There were also recipes that people would share on how to make a "formula" to feed their baby. Unfortunately, these breast milk substitutes weren't very healthy and there was a high infant mortality rate due to malnutrition. [Just a little piece of trivia: The closest animal milk to humans is donkey milk. Because donkeys have never been bred to produce excess milk, it has never been available in a commercial form.]

In the mid-1800s, the first commercially produced formula became available, though it was not widely used. It was not until the 1940s that commercially sold formula became what was prominently used over wet nursing. At this time the market had a few different formulas fighting to be seen as the "miracle pill" moms "needed."

In the late 1950s, breastfeeding started to lose favor with moms and formula became the main way to feed babies. New formulas were heavily marketed to moms as an alternative to breast milk. As more and more babies switched to formula, it became evident that not all babies tolerated the same formula. As science advanced, so did nutrition and infant formula. Formulas began to be developed to tackle problems like an intolerance to lactose (the main sugar in milk), allergies to the protein in milk (casein and whey), and some even more specific problems such as PKU or high calcium. This leaves us today with a wide variety of different brands and types of formulas that are very confusing for parents and physicians alike.

This seems an opportune time to remind you there is a "Why?" in this chapter titled "Why is breast milk best?" Breast milk is best. Don't let shiny labels and marketing campaigns on formula containers cause you to lose sight of that.

Some of the confusion comes with the different brands of formula. In the United States there are four main companies that make commercially available infant formula. Each of these companies have different types of formula to help with specific niches, and each of these brands must have a different name for the different types of formula they sell. The important thing for you to know as a parent is there is actually very little difference from brand to brand. The specific brand would argue that they are very different, and of course that theirs is the best. When you look at the formula contents, the differences are minor and seem to be more for marketing purposes. Remember that all of the store-brand formulas are made by the same company. You can freely buy from one store or another and not worry about upsetting your baby's belly. The only thing that is different about these formulas is the label and the price. By doing some comparison shopping you could save a lot of money as the price could vary quite a bit from one store to another. Don't forget to use those coupons as well.

When starting off feeding your baby a formula, try not to get bogged down in the price or the name or even the description on the label. This is one area in life that more expensive does not indicate better. The most expensive formulas that you will find are made for very specific problems like milk protein allergy and are not the healthiest for most babies. Don't get bogged down in all the symptoms listed on the container. It is your pediatrician's job to make sense of the symptoms. The symptoms for drinking too much or not burping can look very similar to a milk protein allergy to the untrained eye.

Each of the brands will have their main formula, sort of their base model. This is their attempt to get as close to breast milk as possible. No company can claim to be like breast milk, because they just can't duplicate it, but they do try to get as close as they can. This "entry level" formula is the one a pediatrician would recommend that you start with.

Notice that I say your *pediatrician* would recommend. Stop playing doctor! I mean it. Hold up right there.

Do not turn yourself into a nutritionist or even worse a mad scientist.

Do not attempt to interpret your child's gas, fussiness, stooling pattern, or how often they are or aren't hungry as a reason to change formula.

Do.

Not.

Do.

It.

All the variations of formula are not nutritionally equal. Some of the formulas out there are for very specific problems that a baby might have. These problems need to be diagnosed and cared for by your baby's doctor. If you swap out the basic formula for a Soy-Almond blend fortified with Unicorn tears, you may end up doing more harm than good. Babies don't like to change their diet on a whim. Furthermore, these changes can make it even harder for your baby's doctor to figure out what might be wrong with your baby in the event there is a legitimate concern.

TAKE-HOME POINTS:

1. The goal with formula is to choose one as close to breast milk as possible. This is often the basic/entry formula.
2. If your baby is having any issues, be sure to talk to your pediatrician about the problem.
3. Do not just change formulas. Swapping from one basic brand to another basic brand due to availability should be fine. (Again, despite marketing, they're almost the same thing!)
4. Just because it is more expensive, does not make it better!

Why do I need to boil water to make formula?

Now if you are like most people you will actually be surprised by this question. What? Was I supposed to be boiling water to make my baby's formula? No one told me this!

This goes to prove that people do not read the instructions on the back of formula cans. That said, chances are you don't have to worry about boiling your water. But let's first discuss the how's of mixing formula. You need to do it properly or you risk upsetting baby's tummy. There's a lot to cover here. Welcome to formula class. Here we go!

First thing's first, the boiling. The actual instructions are going to say something like, "ask your doctor about the need for cooled, boiled water to mix your formula with."

I saw that. You went and read the formula can and figured out that you've never asked your pediatrician that question. That's okay. That's why I wrote this book. Here's the answer.

When they make the formula at the factory, they have no idea where it will be consumed or what water will be mixed with it. Water quality varies greatly throughout the United States. There's no way they could possibly account for every scenario. There are still places in the United States (believe it or not) that do not have safe drinking water that has been treated and is heavily regulated. Therefore, the formula manufacturer has to assume that there may be a chance that the water you could be mixing with the formula could be contaminated. Boiling water and then allowing it to cool will kill off the harmful bacteria in the water. This avoids the risk of making the baby sick due to bacterial infection. It will only address bacteria, though. Boiling does nothing to other contaminants. That's another item we will get back to in a bit.

Now what does that mean for most of us? Here's the good news.

For the majority of the people living in the United States, we have safe water that has very little risk of any contamination. At the time of this writing, current estimates were that 90 percent of Americans have access to safe, clean, reliable water. As long as you get your water from a safe water source, then you don't need to boil the water before using.

So, who needs to boil water before mixing with the formula?

1. If you are using well water, you should boil your water.
2. If you get water from a cistern or storage system not regulated and regularly tested, you should boil your water.
3. If your city has been listed as a high-risk water area, then you should boil your water before making formula.

Remember that boiling is only going to remove bacteria; it will not remove contaminants

Istock.com/kirilllutz

like lead or mercury. In fact, boiling concentrates these contaminants. As the steam leaves the boiling water, the ratio of contaminants to water increases. If your water is contaminated, do not use the tap water for making formula. For that matter, if your water has these types of contaminants, you shouldn't be drinking it either. Get a filter for your water, or switch to bottled water.

Okay. Let's take a little pause for sanity. This stuff is *boring*! Now you know why nobody reads the instructions and why so many parents are making mistakes in preparing their baby's formula.

When making formula, start with cold water. Warm water can increase the chance of contaminants in your water from the pipes of your house. Warm it up, mix it, then give to baby right away. If you need to boil your water, bring it to a boil for one minute and then allow it to cool. Water that is prepared this way should be used right away and only considered safe for 24 hours.

Did you know that? I will fully admit I didn't know that little fact when preparing formula for my first son. It is a wonder that kiddo survived (by the way, he is nineteen years old and seems to be thriving so I do have proof that you can make mistakes and they still end up fine, but I did try and learn and made fewer mistakes with the next one).

Let's talk about mixing formula. Let's say the instructions say add one scoop to two ounces of water. What do you put in the bottle first, the water, or the powder? Do you think it matters? It does.

If you put in the powder first, then fill up to the 2-ounce mark on the bottle, your mix is off. Remember high school science here. All things have mass, including that powder. So, if you do powder first then fill up to the line, you probably added a half ounce or so less water than you were supposed to. This will cause the formula to be overconcentrated and cause your baby to have a bellyache or possibly increase constipation. Accurate measurements are very important; be sure to read the instructions on the container carefully. Formula ratios are very important for a number of reasons. Measure carefully.

NOTE: In the case of my first child, he ended up getting extremely constipated before I figured out what I was doing wrong. It doesn't seem like much, but it can make a big difference.

TAKE-HOME POINTS:

1. It is important to read the instructions on your formula. There is information on how to properly prepare your baby's formula, how to store the formula, and how to mix the formula safely.

2. Check your water source. If your water is safe, still make sure you are using cold water to mix formula and then warm to desired temperature.

3. If your water source could be contaminated with bacteria, boil it. Start with cold water, bring to a boil for one minute, and then allow to cool down. If your water is contaminated with chemicals or unsafe levels of minerals or metals, then do not use this water to make formula. Filter the water or switch to bottled water.

4. If you're unsure, water testing is inexpensive and easy. I have used Ward Laboratories and was happy with the service. You send them a sample of your water and they test it. In the past they have gotten me results in a week or so via email. Easy!

Why do I need to boil pacifiers, nipples, and bottles?

This question is going to elicit one of three reactions.

The first would be the obvious, "Yes, I'd love to know why I need to boil pacifiers, nipples, and bottles."

The second would be, "Who said I needed to boil pacifiers, nipples, and bottles? Who? Who says so?"

The last would be, "What doctor wrote this book . . . Dr. Pepper? Nobody boils pacifiers, bottles, nipples, or any other baby gear. This sounds crazy."

The funny thing is, all three are valid answers. No matter which of those three reactions most closely matches your own, you can learn something interesting by reading this section.

Istock.com/NegMarDesign

Just for the record: I would have been the second or third person above with my first child. I really thought that the cleanest those bottles, pacifiers, or nipples were going to be were when they came straight out of the package. I had seen what dishes looked like when they came out "clean" from my dishwasher. Also, I always wanted to call a doctor, Dr. Pepper.

Let's just start with the cold, hard facts of what we recommend. We (meaning the collective body of pediatricians) recommend you boil pacifiers, bottles, and nipples prior to first use. You'll want to open the package, wash the item with warm, soapy water, then boil it. For most of you, this will be the last time you need to boil these items. If you live in an area with an unsafe water supply though, then boiling is recommended each time after use. Most pediatricians will also recommend boiling them when your baby has been diagnosed with thrush and continuing until the infection is under control.

Why is it recommended? Well, we have no idea what has happened to that pacifier, bottle, or nipple. Thus, sterilize them and make sure any harmful bacteria that has gotten on them doesn't make its way into your baby. You don't get to examine the factory. You don't know how many or what people have handled the product or the package on its way to you. People these days are crazy. Just remember the little craze that went on when people were taking bites or drinks out

of packages and then putting them back on the shelf. Or even worse, spitting in them and putting them back on the shelf.

How should it be done? It is recommended that you wash the items first in warm, soapy water. Nipples for bottles should be taken apart from the surrounding ring. The items should be put into a clean pan (it would be nice if it was only used for sterilizing baby items, but at the very least extremely clean). They should be submersed in boiling water for at least 5 minutes. Are there other ways to sterilize your items? Absolutely! You can use a steam bottle sterilizer as directed. You can buy a specialized microwave sterilizer and put it into the microwave for about 90 seconds, and you can even find sterilizing tablets that you can add to cold water and allow your bottles, nipples, and pacifiers to soak in.

If you are anything like I was, this is the most thought you have ever given to cleaning a baby bottle. Who would have known that there was a whole science to how you should safely clean and prepare a baby bottle or pacifier?

After the initial sterilizing of the bottles, pacifiers, and nipples, most of you will never do it again. Washing them in hot, soapy water will get the job done perfectly. A dishwasher may do an even better job. Like I mentioned, there are some areas that still require regular sterilization, but if it is recommended to you, do a little digging. You are often being told this because of history, not always because it is true.

TAKE-HOME POINTS:

1. Boil pacifiers, nipples, and bottles after you get them for the first time. Make sure you washed everything in warm soapy water before boiling and using to feed your baby.

2. You should use a clean pan, submerse in boiling water, and leave for 5 minutes. Make sure you use clean utensils to remove from the water to avoid contamination.

3. Boil pacifiers, nipples, and bottles regularly if you have an unsafe water source.

4. Check with your doctor to see if they recommend you boil pacifiers, nipples, or bottles if your baby is being treated for thrush.

5. Pass along the word! Most people are just like you and me. We didn't know how important proper preparation and cleaning of bottles or pacifiers could be. Be sure to tell your family and friends and we can all help keep babies healthier.

Why do people circumcise their baby boys?

Let's just start off this little question with a statement of fact: this topic is going to stir up some feelings. Both sides have their heels firmly dug in and have no intention of giving any ground. Well, I am going to go ahead and irritate both sides by not picking a side.

Yep. You heard me. I am not here to preach or condemn. I am here to give you facts, report the findings, and let you decide on your own. Kind of like the Walter Cronkite of foreskin.

First off, what is a circumcision? Circumcision is a surgical procedure to remove the foreskin that covers the tip or glans of the penis. It is usually performed at 2 to 3 days of age if done in the hospital here in the United States. In traditional Judaism, it is performed ceremoniously on the eighth day from birth. The foreskin is split and the adhesions that stick it to the head of the penis are removed. Finally, the excess skin covering the head of the penis is surgically removed or clamped off so it will fall off. It usually takes 3 to 5 days for it to completely heal.

Why is circumcision even a thing? That is a good question. Like, who is the first person that looked at a penis and thought, "hmmmm ... okay. I like it, but it needs work. What if I ... " The first man to volunteer for that procedure was either very brave, or very stupid. Possibly both.

I can tell you it has been around for a long time. The first documented evidence of circumcision goes back to about 2400 BC in the Egyptians. It is a well-documented procedure in the Jewish culture as well. Throughout the ages, circumcision was seen as a religious ritual or in some cultures as a coming of age ritual. It has gone in and out of favor throughout the centuries.

Skipping through all the history books and religious texts, why is it still being done today? Mostly it is still being done for religious and cultural reasons. Recently, however, the AAP and the WHO stepped in and gave some scientific and health-based reasoning for the procedure. They did stop short of universally recommending circumcisions. They stated that it does have the ability to decrease urinary tract infections, decrease the spread of sexually transmitted diseases, and decrease the incidence of penile cancer.

What does that mean to you and your baby?

Probably not much, unless you are already planning on the procedure and wanting a medical justification. I will tell you that I have been involved in the care of babies since I was in medical school in the late 1990s. I have seen a full circle when it comes to male circumcision. When I started, it was just largely accepted as something that was done as a choice, again largely for religious or cultural reasons. Then it came out as something that was done despite having no medical justification for doing it. Soon after that, it became the norm to not recommend it be done. Then

it came back full circle and they were recommending it be done again.

Trust me when I tell you, it will change again. When it comes to your baby, just know that there are medical reasons to circumcise, and there are medical reasons not to circumcise. Which leaves you right where you started.

What should you do with your baby?

This is exactly what I think circumcision should be. It is a decision that you should make based on your beliefs, your customs, and your desires. Make the decision for the right reasons and you will be justified in your decision.

There are a couple of things that you should know about each direction that you could go. If you choose to leave your son intact or uncircumcised, leave it alone. Do not try to pull back the foreskin so you can see the tip or glans of the penis. The foreskin is stuck to the head of the penis with adhesions and these can tear with excess force and cause pain and swelling. Gently pull the foreskin taut and wash with soap and water when bathing. You may see a white, chalky substance come out occasionally that is called "smegma." It is just old, dead skin cells and not anything to worry about. Keep it washed with soap and water, and all should be well.

If you choose to circumcise your son, the first 3 to 5 days after the procedure, the head of the penis will be covered in a yellowish-green slime. This is its version of a scab and is the way that it heals. You will want to use some Vaseline on the penis or diaper to keep the head of the penis from sticking to the diaper. Once the circumcision has healed, you will want to pull the foreskin back with each diaper change until you can see the ridge around the edge of the glans of the penis to prevent it from forming adhesions and getting stuck.

TAKE-HOME POINTS:

1. Circumcision has been performed for thousands of years for mostly cultural and religious reasons.
2. Medically, the reasons to justify circumcision are reductions in urinary tract infections, sexually transmitted diseases, and penile cancer.
3. Make sure whatever you choose to do with your child that you feel comfortable with the decision. Do not feel like you are being forced to do something you think is wrong.
4. Remember to take different approaches to cleaning and caring for their penis depending on whether they are circumcised or not. You do not take care of them the same way.

Why are cold sores so scary for babies?

Talk about a topic coming completely out of the blue. Cold sores? Huh? Here we are in the section of the book that is revolving around topics to think about before a baby is born, and out of nowhere comes the topic of cold sores. You've got to wonder, what was he drinking that morning when he sat down in front of his computer?

Trust me, there is a method to my madness, and to my timing. So yes. Let's talk about the much-maligned and seldom properly understood cold sore.

First, let's start off with an explanation of the simple cold sore. You have seen them your whole life. That little crusty sore that shows up on your lip or in the corner of your mouth. They last several days and just look ugly. They also have an image that radiates pain. They look painful, like looking at something and saying "dang . . . that looks like it hurts!" Well, yeah . . . they do hurt. These are different from the also common canker sore, which is a painful ulcer on the inside of the mouth but are completely benign.

If you have one, they start off with a little tingle or burning feeling and then form a little pimple-like bump that quickly becomes an ulcer. That ulcer can crack, bleed, ooze goo, and all sorts of distasteful things. Ewwww. They are zero fun to deal with. If infected, you'll rush straight to the corner drugstore and buy whatever they're selling to cure it,

at whatever price it is. You ever notice you don't see ads for cold sore medication? You know why? Because cold sores suck, that's why. They don't need to advertise; if you've got one, you'll buy the cure. No further motivation is required!

Also, if you have had them before, you may have realized something else about cold sores. They tend to appear when you are stressed out. You tend to get one when you are on your period, when you have been sick, when you haven't had enough sleep, or when you are just really stressed out to your breaking point . . . and . . . *Bam*! Let's add a little cold sore to the mix. It's nature's way of reminding you things can always get worse.

If any of this sounds familiar, then you are going to understand the timing of this little topic. What is going to happen when you have a baby? You are going to be stressed out, you are going to be tired, and your hormones are going to be shifting all over the place. Now even though you aren't sick, you might as well be with as much as your body has just gone through. The perfect time to break out with a cold sore is right after you have a baby.

Cold sores are caused by one of the herpes viruses, Herpes Simplex Type 1. The sound of the word herpes gets everybody agitated because of the herpes spread as a sexually transmitted disease. Cold sores aren't the same, but they are related.

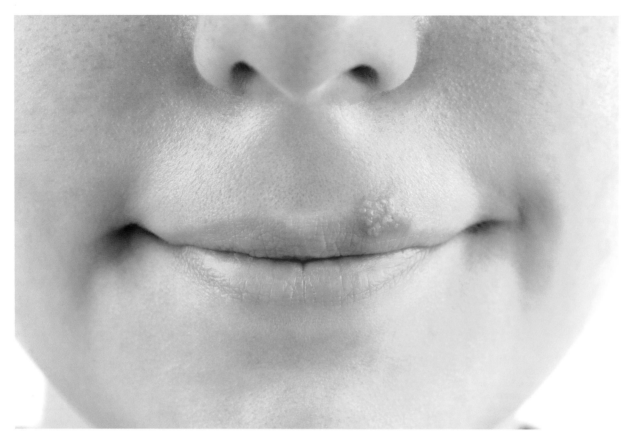

Istock.com/LeventKonuk

What people don't realize is that herpes is a whole family of viruses. These viruses include herpes virus type 1 that causes cold sores and herpes virus type 2, which traditionally causes the STD "herpes." There's also herpes-zoster that causes chicken pox and shingles, the Epstein-Barr virus that causes mononucleosis, and multiple others.

Herpes simplex type 1, the virus causing the common cold sore, is spread by direct contact with a lesion and allowed access to the body via a break in the mucous membrane or skin. For most people exposed to the virus, nothing happens. They don't have a break in the mucous membrane or skin, and it causes no infection. Others may get exposed and their body develops antibodies to the virus and they never have a breakout. Others may just get the occasional cold sore. This is all incredibly *boring* and you still can't see why this needs to even be a question. What is even the point? Why is this in the book, much less here in the beginning of the book?

Herpes simplex type 1 has the potential to kill your baby! There, I said it. Now you know why it is in the book, why it is at the front, and why that little cold sore virus scares pediatricians. If a baby is exposed to the herpes virus, be it from type 1 or type 2, they have the potential to have severe infections from it. Their infections can fall into one of three main categories.

The first type of infection is the least severe and is called SEM. The S is for skin, E is for eyes, and M is for mouth. They could get a classic blistering rash on their skin, an infection in the eyes which can lead to corneal scarring and vision problems, or a terrible rash in their mouth known as herpetic gingivostomatitis. The gingivostomatitis is the most common manifestation and will be extremely painful but then will lead to a lifetime of breaking out in cold sores on the lips afterward. Remember how we discussed the crappiness of cold sores? So yes, the best-case scenario here is a painful rash that leads to a lifetime of nasty lip infections that hurt. It goes downhill from there.

The second type is encephalitis. This is where the infection manifests itself in the brain. This will usually show up as seizures or altered consciousness in a newborn. The virus itself just destroys the cells that it infects so it can destroy parts of the brain that unfortunately can't grow back. I have had two cases of this in my career—one that was caused by a mom with vaginal herpes and one that was caused by a grandma who had a cold sore kissing the newborn. This is a terrible outcome and a very problematic infection.

The third type is disseminated herpes and causes a debilitating infection involving the entire body. It can lead to multi-organ shutdown and requires intensive care and lots of prayer to get through. It has a 50 percent survival rate. The good news is that it has great prognosis if they survive. Unfortunately, the only one I have had didn't survive. I pray I never see another one.

The whole purpose of this "Why" is to scare you about a simple cold sore. Yes, I am actively using a scare tactic. I am okay with that given the potential harm to your baby if they become infected. Don't let people kiss your baby. If anyone is showing a visible cold sore, don't expose the baby to them at all. If you know you have had cold sores in the past, be aware of the symptoms. If you are feeling like you are going to break out, DO NOT kiss your baby.

TAKE-HOME POINTS:

1. Cold sores are caused by Herpes simplex 1 and can cause severe infections in babies.
2. Don't let anyone who has a cold sore kiss or handle your baby.
3. If you have had cold sores in the past, know that having a baby is a perfect storm to cause another one.
4. It's a great idea to not let people kiss your baby. Them being offended is a small price to pay for your child's safety.
5. This is a minor irritating infection for an adult, but possibly fatal for your baby. Please take it very, VERY seriously.

PART 2
NEWBORN
(The first three to five days)

"If your baby is 'beautiful and perfect, never cries or fusses, sleeps on schedule and burps on demand, an angel all the time,' you're the grandma."

—*Theresa Bloomingdale*

Istock.com/damircudic

Why does my newborn get a vitamin K shot?

Every once in a while, we as mankind get the sudden urge to reinvent the wheel. This has seemed to happen the last several years with the vitamin K shot. There have been lots of articles written on the Internet.

Due to this resurgence of snake oil sales, there have been several parents who decline the vitamin K shot at birth. Suddenly we start to see a resurgence in the complications from vitamin K deficiency to remind us of why the

Istock.com/ratmaner

shot was given in the first place. Weird how that works, huh?

So, the question remains: Why do we give a vitamin K shot?

Vitamin K is an essential fat-soluble vitamin that is required in the clotting pathway. Simply put, it is needed for us to be able to effectively stop bleeding. Vitamin K is not passed through the placenta very well and therefore most newborns are deficient at birth. Complications are seen with vitamin K deficiency at three different ages.

The first is early vitamin K deficient bleeding, which occurs in the first day of life. It is defined as severe bleeding internally in the abdominal cavity or in the brain. It is usually very serious and is almost exclusively seen in mothers who were taking a medication for seizures or tuberculosis.

The second way in which it can show up is known as Classical Vitamin K Deficient Bleeding. This issue occurs from day one to seven. It is characterized by excessive bruising, oozing from umbilical stumps, bleeding from circumcision sites, and internal bleeding.

The third manner is known as Late Onset Vitamin K Deficient Bleeding. This problem occurs between two to twelve weeks of age, and sometimes up to six months of age. It is usually severe and often causes bleeding into the brain. This is almost exclusively seen in babies who did not receive the vitamin K shot at birth and are exclusively breastfed.

Okay, vitamin K good, no vitamin K bad. So, what is the controversy and why are we even talking about this?

There are some people who are just against anything that isn't natural. Several "experts" have expressed concern about the trauma a baby feels from the shot at birth and how that can affect them growing up. They also worry about the risk of infection the needle might pose or how it might affect breastfeeding. Some even worry that the injection poses too high a risk of potential toxins or that the dose is too high. They realize that vitamin K is needed, but they don't like the delivery system. They recommend the use of oral vitamin K.

I guess the next logical question should be, does the oral vitamin K work? The answer would be . . . kind of. Remember up above when we said there are three types of vitamin K deficient bleeding? Well, the early kind is not affected by the oral vitamin K or the shot. It is caused by a deficiency from the mom being on a medication and the bleed happens at birth. It's a bit late for preventative measures, unfortunately.

For the second type—or Classical Vitamin Deficient Bleeding—the oral and the injected vitamin K are equally as effective. Yay!

The problem comes from that third type, the Late Onset Vitamin K Deficient Bleeding. It is only helped with the injectable vitamin K.

So why is this even a question? Why wouldn't everyone just get the vitamin K shot and not have to worry about their baby having Late Onset Vitamin K Deficient Bleeding?

Luckily, most parents elect to give their baby the vitamin K shot, but there are a few that refuse. That number has increased as the Internet has allowed more voices to be heard and gullible people to be convinced about things that lack validation. Since the beginning of time, there have been alternative medicines and cures. Not all of them are nonsensical gibberish, but the rise of the information age has made it difficult to sort the good from the bad. I guess it's the law of unintended consequences at work.

The old-time medicine man didn't have a medicine that would cure you, but boy did he ever have an advertising pitch that would convince you. Since alcohol was the main ingredient in snake oil cocktails a century or so ago, I am sure taking it made you feel . . . something. Or maybe nothing.

Yet, with all the advancements we have made, that medicine man can still be heard and can still convince people. Only these days he's not peddling from the foldout of his stagecoach, and the miracle pills aren't for sale in the general store next to the dried pork and bullets. Today, it is clicks and likes and shares. Today the charmers use Facebook and the Internet to pitch their different ideas. Some of them have genuine info to share, while others are selling pure hooey. The ratio *greatly* swings toward manure, unfortunately.

Give mankind a few decades, and maybe we'll figure this information-sharing thing out. For now, here's some great advice.

TAKE-HOME POINTS:

1. Vitamin K is an essential fat-soluble vitamin that is required for blood to clot.
2. Vitamin K deficiency in the newborn can lead to bleeding from the umbilical stump, circumcision, or needle pokes in the first seven days of life or can have a late onset that can lead to strokes, internal bleeding, and death.
3. Oral vitamin K can prevent the Classical Vitamin K Deficient Bleeding, but not the Late Onset Vitamin K Deficient Bleeding, which is the most severe.
4. The vitamin K shot at birth is the gold standard for preventing Vitamin K Deficient Bleeding.
5. Be careful about what you read on the Internet or who you listen to. Always ask the question, is the person giving the advice going to be with you or help you if they are wrong?

Why does my newborn get a hepatitis B shot?

Isn't hepatitis B that virus you get from sex or sharing needles when doing drugs? Why on earth would we ever want to give a brand-new baby a vaccine that they won't need until they are older? Let's just be honest, my baby is pure as the newly fallen snow and will never need to be protected because they aren't going to do anything wrong, *ever! Not my baby!*

If all that were true, we would still need to give the hepatitis B vaccine at birth. Unfortunately, that isn't the way it really happens. There is good reason for it, and the vaccine is working. We see the results in real-world data. Let me show you.

First, you are going to need to know some basic facts about hepatitis B.

Hepatitis B is a virus that infects the liver. It has two phases. First, there is an acute phase when you initially acquire the virus. Next comes a chronic phase where it just decides to hang around forever and make you feel bad for the rest of your life. The problem with the chronic phase is that it can progress to liver cirrhosis, liver failure, and even liver cancer. Obviously, we want to avoid that if we can.

Hepatitis B can be spread by blood and infected body fluids. This allows it to be spread by sexual contact and contaminated needles. Less nefarious sources like sharing razors or toothbrushes can also spread the virus. So, it can be passed through blood or fluids, and through inanimate objects that have been contaminated. Here's the kicker—it can also be spread at birth from an infected mother. Now, you can see how your baby could be as pure as the driven snow and still get infected with hepatitis B.

The acute phase of hepatitis B can last up to six months. Sometimes the patient will have no symptoms at all. Other times there may be some mild abdominal pain and aching. In rare cases it can become acute hepatitis with severe abdominal pain, vomiting, diarrhea, fever, and dehydration that can lead to hospitalization.

The chronic phase of hepatitis B is when symptoms last longer than six months after the initial infection. They could last anywhere from six months to a lifetime. Symptoms could range from very little, to slowly developing cirrhosis of the liver and liver failure. Some cases even result in liver cancer. Chronic hepatitis B leads to over 2000 deaths per year in the United States alone.

Here's the real rub. The chance of developing chronic hepatitis B is different depending on the age that you were exposed to the virus. If you were given the hepatitis B virus from your mother at birth, the chance of developing chronic hepatitis B is 90 percent. If you are infected from the ages of two to five, it is about 30 percent. If you are infected as an adult, it falls to about 5 percent. Thirty to forty percent of all adults suffering from chronic hepatitis B acquired it in childhood.

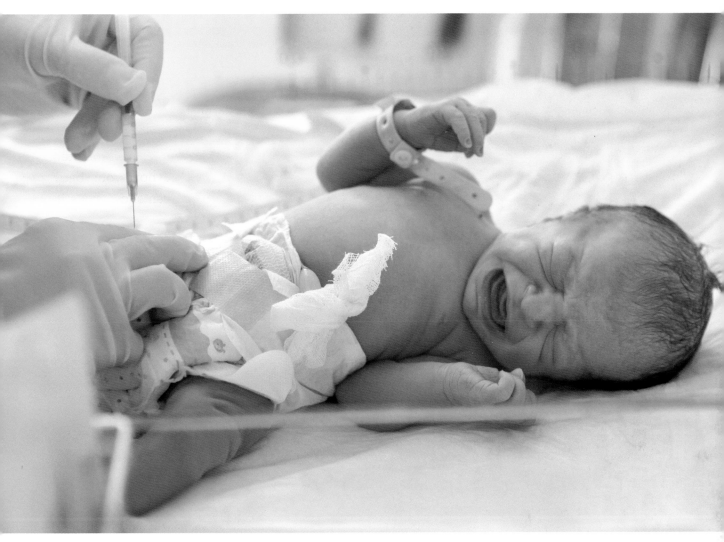

Istock.com/Coral222

Wait. Don't we test moms for hepatitis B when they are pregnant?

Some moms are tested for hepatitis B when they have their first OB/Gyn visit. The problem is that not all moms are tested, and some tests will be false negative because the moms have not been infected for a long enough time. Moms also can become unknowingly infected after the testing, but before the baby is actually born. Remember—it's not all dark spooky behaviors featured on late night B movies that spread this virus. Also remember the bit about the age you are exposed. You could borrow a razor from Aunt Sally, but you never knew Aunt Sally had some pretty serious closet skeletons and a case of hep B. Being a grown-up means you have decent odds that you catch the virus and never know it because you have zero symptoms, ever.

If we know that a mom has hepatitis B before the baby is born, we give the baby a hepatitis B vaccine at birth as well as a dose of hepatitis B immunoglobulin to prevent the baby from developing hepatitis B. The amazing thing is that if we don't know mom's hepatitis B status and the baby is exposed to hepatitis B by her and gets just the vaccine, the vaccine will prevent them from developing chronic hepatitis B.

Hopefully now it is starting to become clearer. The most important time to get the hepatitis B vaccine is at birth. This is where they have the highest chance of developing chronic hepatitis B.

Remember I told you the vaccine was working, and we can prove it?

Since the hepatitis B vaccine was introduced in the United States, the annual cases of hepatitis B have been falling. In the parts of the world where the vaccine is not administered, they are steadily increasing.

Modern science wins again!

I hope to see this simple, effective safety measure widely applied, and soon. Until that becomes a reality, here are the take-home points:

TAKE-HOME POINTS:

1. Hepatitis B is a virus that is spread by blood and infected bodily fluids. It can be spread by infected needles, sexual contact, toothbrushes, and accidental needle sticks. A mom can pass it to her baby at birth.

2. Hepatitis B vaccine will prevent a baby that is unknowingly exposed to hepatitis B from developing chronic hepatitis B.

3. The most important time to protect your baby from hepatitis B is at birth.

Why do they put antibiotic ointment in my baby's eyes?

Because it's the law!

Well, that is one answer, but it is a little more complicated than that. It is the law in most states in the United States to apply antibiotic ointment to a baby's eyes soon after they are born. The reason is to prevent eye infections that can lead to blindness. In fact, congenital infection of the eyes was one of the leading causes of blindness.

The antibiotic is mostly to prevent congenital infections of the eye from chlamydia and gonorrhea, although it will also prevent

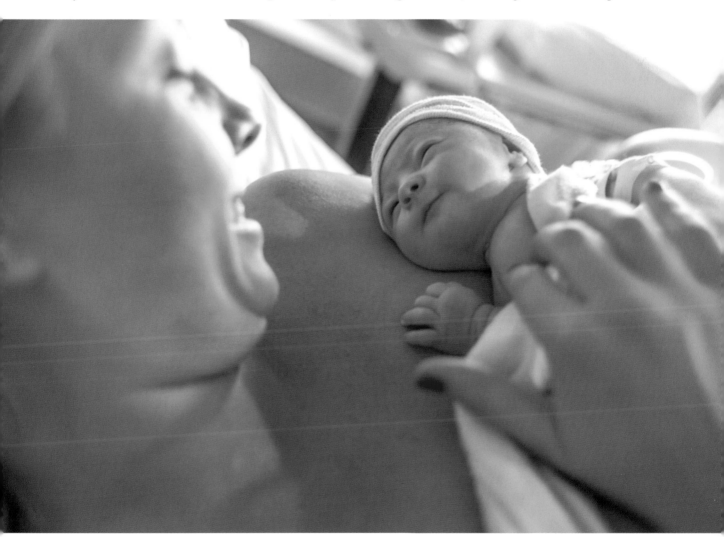

Istock.com/AleMoraes244

infections with E. coli. Now those first two names may sound familiar as two very common sexually transmitted diseases. These STDs are present in the birthing canal during birth and can infect the baby's eyes as they are being born. E. coli is a bacterium found in the GI tract and can also be acquired during the birthing process.

Congenital infections of the eye are nothing to joke about. In the 1800s, infections of the eye at birth due to gonorrhea were responsible for over half of the cases of blindness. Learning to diagnose and treat congenital infections of the eye was a huge step in preventing blindness. The next huge step was treating with antibiotics to prevent it from happening at all, also known as prophylaxis.

There is a little history that we need to talk about here. Before routine prenatal screening, chlamydia or gonorrhea in the pregnant mom was one of those things that we might or might not know about. Unless they had symptoms or complained about something, it might not be found during pregnancy. About thirty years ago it became very common to screen newly pregnant moms for both chlamydia and gonorrhea. If they tested positive, they and their partners were treated and then the pregnant mom was retested to make sure the infection was gone. Many argue that because of this testing there is very little reason to still treat the newborns. There are still a few little wrinkles though.

We test fairly early in pregnancy, so a mom might get infected by her partner after the test had been done and think she was clear. Humans being humans, infidelity can also lead to an infection that happens after

mom is screened. Trust me, these things have happened over the years! There are also women who don't get tested because it either got missed in the screening process, the test got lost, or they didn't have adequate prenatal care. By putting the antibiotic ointment in all babies' eyes, we don't miss anyone. It's so easy, and if not done we could have a case of blindness that should have easily been prevented.

If it can prevent blindness, why in the world would anyone ever be against it? Well, it can make their vision very blurry for an hour or so. It is thought that this could interfere with a baby bonding with her mom and cause problems with breastfeeding. There are also people who are very much in favor of doing things "naturally" and worry about the toxicity of the antibiotic to the baby.

This is one of those rare times that I'm going to jump in with my opinion. I completely understand the side that wants to not give any medicine if it is not needed. I see the change in screenings over the years and I understand that in a scheduled C-section there is no chance of getting an infection from the birth canal. I also come from the pediatric side where one case of preventable blindness is one too many.

I think there is an acceptable truce in the middle.

Just wait a couple of hours before giving the baby the eye ointment. Let the baby have a chance to see mommy, breastfeed, and look around a bit. Then give the baby the eye ointment when they normally go to sleep anyway. We still give the baby an antibiotic they may not need, but if it prevents the eye infection that could leave them permanently blind, I feel it's worth it. The slight delay gives the baby the ability to bond and breastfeed without blurred vision. It makes the timing a little harder on the nurses in the hospital, but it takes care of a lot of people's problems with our current paradigm.

I also see no problem in people making good educated decisions. "My baby was born via C-section . . . I don't want her to have the antibiotic" makes sense to me. Sometimes when laws start covering things, they leave little room for intelligent decisions to be made.

TAKE-HOME POINTS:

1. The antibiotic ointment given to a baby at birth is to prevent eye infections acquired in the birth canal.
2. These infections can be due to sexually transmitted diseases as well as bacteria normally found in the gastrointestinal tract.
3. Congenital conjunctivitis used to be a huge cause of blindness and visual loss.
4. I believe with a little common sense and a "birth plan" you can bond with your baby, breastfeed, and still get the antibiotic treatment done.
5. I think you can make a good educated decision and avoid the antibiotic eye treatment if you know your baby has no risk of getting an infection, like being born via a C-section.

Why did my baby have his heel poked in the hospital?

There are several ways that you can draw blood from a baby. Each has a different reason for doing it that way, and different technical amounts of expertise to perform.

A heel stick is technically the easiest to perform and can be done by nurses, phlebotomists, and physicians. It is a fairly painful way to get blood. It has limitations in the amount of blood you can obtain this way, and it can be contaminated with normal skin bacteria, making it useless for drawing blood for cultures. The blood sample can be affected by too much squeezing of the heel, causing the red blood cells to break and increase potassium levels or lowering the number of red blood cells seen on the test. This type of blood draw is primarily done on newborns when a small sample size is needed.

Venipuncture is another method commonly used to draw blood. It requires a little more technical expertise. It can be performed by nurses, phlebotomists, and physicians. It can be used

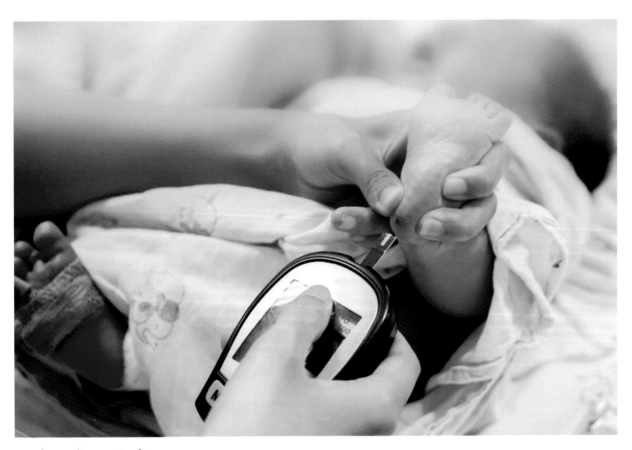

Istock.com/Atiwat Studio

to draw larger amounts of blood for most tests needed in medicine, like to fill a small vial. This is the preferred method to draw blood for most tests done in babies and adults. It increases in difficulty when multiple attempts have been tried before, as sites can bruise. Bruising makes it harder to get blood from that area again, or be able to start an IV in that area.

Arterial blood draw is the least common way to draw blood and is usually done by a respiratory therapist or physician. This can be used for large amounts of blood unable to be drawn from another site, but mostly is used to look at blood gases when a patient is having difficulty breathing or is on a ventilator. Due to higher pressure in an artery, side effects from this type of blood draw are much higher.

So back to the question: Why are they sticking my baby's heel in the hospital?

For the vast majority of babies born without any illness or complications, the heel poke is for screening. In the United States there are several tests that are done to look for hard to diagnose and rare conditions. These samples are sent to a state lab, and the results are sent back to the hospital or pediatrician. These tests vary state to state and typically include testing for things like cystic fibrosis, sickle cell anemia, congenital hypothyroidism, or galactosemia. The reason for performing these tests is because if a condition is identified early, we can dramatically improve things for your baby. Simple changes in the type of milk a baby drinks or adding a medicine can dramatically change the overall outcome for the baby.

For example, in the case of congenital hypothyroidism, early diagnosis can lead to starting thyroid hormone early and preventing a terrible condition known as cretinism. When the diagnosis was delayed these babies would develop changes in their tongue, facial abnormalities, poor growth, and mental retardation. Hypothyroidism in babies is uncommon, but I have seen three of them in my twenty-year career. By simply knowing the diagnosis early, these babies can be started on a lifelong medication that will prevent the abnormalities from happening.

In the case of babies who are born to diabetic mothers, their heel sticks may be used to look at blood sugars as well. Most hospitals will have a protocol in place to follow infants of diabetic mothers to make sure that their blood sugar is not getting dangerously low.

If a baby appears to be ill, then the heel poke may be done to get a small sample of blood to run a CBC (complete blood count), which alerts a doctor to the presence of infection and whether it is viral or bacterial.

It's important to note that large amounts of blood are unable to be obtained this way and there is a risk of contamination. Therefore, blood for cultures can't be drawn this way.

Finally, one of the more common reasons that a newborn will have a heel poke is to test for bilirubin levels. There are ways to screen for bilirubin levels through the skin, but they're not the most reliable. Before any therapeutic decisions are made, the doctor will always want a blood bilirubin test. Depending on the level found, if the baby is looking jaundiced, a baby could have several heel pokes to monitor their bilirubin level. For more information on bilirubin and jaundice please read the chapter on "Why did my baby become jaundiced?"

TAKE-HOME POINTS:

1. Heel pokes are an easy way to obtain blood from a baby that requires very little expertise and preserves veins that might be needed for larger blood draws or for IV access.
2. Heel pokes are used to obtain newborn screens, check blood sugar, monitor bilirubin levels, and even check initial CBC blood tests.
3. Little ones get over the slight pinch pretty quickly; a heel poke is a very helpful tool and minimally invasive.

Why are my baby's hands and feet turning purple?

So, one thing we can agree on—purple or blue skin is bad, right? It's common knowledge. If you are turning blue or purple, things just got serious, right?

We all know that blue or purple skin is the opposite of healthy skin. We are taught that it has something to do with a heart problem and happens right before somebody is going to die. This is agreed-upon information in our culture.

Then this happens . . .

Istock.com/Satoshi-K

Here you are a brand-new parent. When I say brand-new, I mean brand-new as when the echo of the first cry is still bouncing around the corners of the room. There's this incredible rush of emotions as they hand you your little bundle of joy. You're thrilled, scared, overjoyed, in pain, and possibly a little medicated. It's safe to say this is one of the most vulnerable moments you'll ever share with a bunch of medical professionals. Then, radiating with happiness, you look at your gorgeous, amazing child . . .

And . . . his feet are blue.

WHAT!?!

Now, nobody seems alarmed and you are surrounded by medical people. Surely, they see this, right? You hold your baby for a few more minutes and now his hands are blue and his lower legs are blue. Still no one is freaking out. You'd like to freak out, but frankly freaking out can be exhausting and it's been a long day. Still, that blue skin is alarming to look at.

So why is it happening? What's going on here?

Let's go back and look at that blue-colored skin. The blue-colored skin is called cyanosis. It is caused by low oxygen levels in the blood. It can be caused by congenital heart defects or respiratory distress in the newborn.

Wait a second! Those are terrible things for a baby to have, so why aren't these medical people freaking out over the fact that my precious baby has blue hands and feet? The news stories are true; medicine has gotten terrible and no one really cares anymore.

Nope, that's not it. Read on.

There is another little thing that will cause cyanosis in the newborn and that is being cold. How can being cold cause cyanosis? First, we need to divide cyanosis into two categories. There is central cyanosis and peripheral cyanosis. Peripheral cyanosis is blueness that happens at the farthest distance from the heart. Central cyanosis is blueness close to the heart or what we will call our core or middle.

A newborn doesn't have a lot of fat to act as insulation to maintain their body temperature. If the air around them is cold and they don't have enough clothes or blankets to keep them warm, their body temperature will start to drop rapidly. There are certain areas that are more important to keep warm. These areas include the heart, lungs, intestines, and brain. It is less important that we keep the hands and feet warm. Because of this, a baby's body clamps down the blood vessels delivering blood to the hands and feet in order to shunt more blood to the middle of its body. This results in his or her hands and feet turning purple and feeling a little cold to the touch.

Trust me, those medical professionals all around you and your baby know that blue is bad. They have already made sure that the baby's heart and lungs are sounding good and that the inside of their mouth looks nice and red. They checked; you likely didn't notice. The checks take a few seconds and you're having quite the moment, after all. If all those things are good then they can be fairly confident that your baby's blue hands and feet are just due to the baby being cold. This is another great reason to get baby right next to mom's skin as soon as possible after birth.

A good rule of thumb when it comes to keeping a baby warm enough to prevent the hands and feet from turning blue is to make sure the baby is wearing one layer more of clothes or covering than you are comfortable wearing.

Why does poop have different colors?

Little did I know that I was going to go through four years of college, four years of medical school, and three years of residency in order for me to become a pediatrician and I was doing all that to become an expert in poop. You ever start a job or a career and end up doing something daily you had no idea was going to be a part of it? That's my relationship with poop. I'm not going to imbue you with *all* of the poop knowledge I have. After all, I worked hard for it, and who knows when my poop skills will be in demand.

Nevertheless, you were kind enough to buy my book, so I will share *some* poop secrets with you. To start off, it is probably just a good idea to go through the evolution of poop.

The first several stools that a baby has are called meconium. These look like black tar, and they also stick to your baby like tar. The good news is that you don't have to deal with it for long. This type of stool will only last the first few days. Meconium is made up of some amniotic fluid, skin cells, hair, bile, blood, and intestinal secretions. As your baby transitions to life outside the womb, these things will leave her system and the meconium will cease to be. While it looks pretty gross, it actually doesn't smell as bad as what is coming.

The next type of stool that a baby will have we call transitional stools. I realize it isn't incredibly creative; it shows up between

Istock.com/macida

42

days two and four of life. It gets its name from the fact that we are transitioning from meconium to normal baby stools. This type of poop can range from dark green to lighter green and even have some yellow streaks or flecks. It smells . . . well . . . you might want to ensure proper ventilation.

Next, we get to the classic newborn poop. This shows up once he has been eating well for a couple of days and will be what his stool looks like for most of the first month. I usually like to compare poop to foods I don't really like. I tell parents that this poop will look like watery, yellowish-green cottage cheese (sorry if I've ruined cottage cheese for you forever). Feel free to substitute a food description using food you do not like. I have yet to see poop that resembles cheeseburgers or pizza, so I think we're safe there. If your baby is breastfed, it will tend to be more yellow-colored. If they are formula fed, it tends to be greener and sometimes even brown.

Around the time a baby is a month old he will start to stool less frequently, ranging from one to two times per day to even skipping days in between pooping. Because of this, more water is absorbed from the stool and the poop tends to get a little darker in color. Still the breastfed baby's poop will be lighter colored than that of the formula-fed babies.

Next comes the poop we see when he starts eating food. Holy cow, this stuff can *stink*. It can come out all kinds of colors now. It's like the world's smelliest kaleidoscope. Don't freak out if the color of the poop has no correlation with the color of food going into him. You can't feed him specific things

to produce less smelly or uniformly colored poop. It doesn't really work that way.

At this point I like to tell parents that there are only three colors of poop that I worry about. I don't want to see red, black, or white stools. Red and black both make us worry about blood and we will need to find out why we have blood in our stools. White stools may indicate that the baby isn't absorbing fat the way they should. This could indicate an underlying medical problem and can also affect how well a baby will grow. So basically, any color or smell except red, black or white is fine (well, okay, it may not be fine to smell, but somehow the babies never seem to mind).

The important thing to know is that poop is going to change colors and that is perfectly okay and normal. It will change as they grow, and it can change depending on what kinds of foods they are eating. It can change because one day the baby may have needed different types of nutrients than she did yesterday, so she absorbed or got rid of different things. Smells might literally stink but aren't worrisome either.

TAKE-HOME POINTS:

1. Stools will change color depending on the baby's age, food, and needs.
2. The colors of stool that we worry about are red, black, and white.
3. Remember your pediatrician is an expert in poop. If you are worried, always just ask. We may never have known we were going to have this information, but have it we do, and we're happy to share.

Why is my newborn snoring?

You have a baby and both of you are exhausted. The planets have aligned and somehow the baby is fed, changed, in bed, and drifting asleep at the exact time that you are ready to go to sleep as well. You are snuggling into bed and are just about to drift off to peaceful, well-deserved slumber and all of a sudden, a loud snoring sound starts coming from your newborn.

Do you panic?

Should you panic?

Should your newborn be sounding like she is mowing down the 100 Acre Wood, in Winnie the Pooh, with a chainsaw?

Now that moment when you could have drifted off is ruined. You are wondering if your baby is getting sick, having some kind of problem breathing, or is this that sleep apnea that the TV is always talking about? Does my baby need that adjustable bed or one of those fancy pillows?

Calm down, this is all okay and you should get some of that well-deserved sleep. I try to cut this panic moment off the first time I talk to new parents just to keep them calm. Most of us in the United States like a climate-controlled house. Because of this, we

Istock.com/LSOphoto

tend to run central heat and air units most of the time. Most of these units tend to dry out the moisture in our houses, making the air in the house dry. As a baby is breathing this dry air through their nose it tends to make the mucus in their nose and throat thicker. As the baby goes to sleep, the muscles around their airway also relax and naturally make the airway a little narrower. The mucus starts moving up and down the narrower airway as the baby breathes in and out and *Bam*! Suddenly there is a snoring baby and a parent who is awake and worried.

For the most part, it is just a noise. As long as it isn't bothering the baby, you shouldn't allow it to bother you. There are of course some exceptions.

If your baby is not liking the congestion and it is keeping the baby from sleeping well, you can run a cool mist humidifier next to the baby. This will increase the humidity of the air the baby is breathing. The humidified air will dry up the mucous membranes less, causing mucus to be thinner and resulting in less snoring.

Remember that apnea thing? That is something we worry about in all people, not just babies. If your baby has respiratory pauses where they are stopping breathing, then we have a problem. The official definition of apnea is a respiratory pause that lasts more than 20 seconds. I tell parents that if they notice a pause of 15 seconds, let me know. Chances are if you are noticing a 15-second pause, there is a 20-second pause in there somewhere that you are missing.

The other area of concern would be if your baby is sick and is now making the snoring sound. As long as it is just the noise, then everything is still fine. But if you notice that your baby is breathing faster, looking like it is hard to breathe, or uncomfortable, then your baby has more of a problem than just a snore and it's time to let your doctor earn their keep.

TAKE-HOME POINTS:

1. Neonatal congestion is very common. It is the most likely reason your baby is snoring.
2. If the congestion is bothering your baby and keeping him from sleeping well, you can run a humidifier next to him and see if it helps.
3. If your baby is acting sick, has a fever, or is working to breathe, then you need to contact your doctor.
4. If the snoring is *only* noise with no other complications whatsoever, then it is probably fine. Go back to sleep.

Why is there orange stuff in my newborn's pee?

There are some things that happen at a very specific time and never again. This is one of those. Orange stuff in the pee is going to be a one and done occurrence that always happens around the time your baby is between two and five days old. It is very common and rarely is it anything to worry about.

First off, what is it actually going to look like? You will see a brick-orange, orange, or even slight red-tinged color in the front part of the diaper. Most parents will jump to the conclusion that it is blood. I think that is only because blood is the first thing that comes to mind and parenting involves a certain amount of panic. If you look at it closely, it looks nothing like blood at all.

What is it? Well, the color is caused by urate crystals. Urate crystals are caused by uric acid. Uric acid is a normal byproduct that our body produces and then is excreted by our kidneys and in our stool. In the first several days of life, a baby may not be drinking enough fluids. This is especially true in breastfed babies whose needs outpace mom's ability to produce. Due to not getting enough fluids the baby gets a little dehydrated and starts to try and lose less fluids in urine and stool. This will cause the urine to become more concentrated. As the urine gets more concentrated it will get darker and you will be able to see things like the urate crystals. These are always present, but when urine is at proper dilution you won't notice.

Do you need to worry? Most of the time this is nothing to worry about. You will see the urate crystals in a diaper or two, the baby starts drinking more milk, the baby becomes better hydrated, urine becomes less concentrated, and pee is back to just pee colored. In the breast milk example above, nature will catch up, just give it a day or two.

If the orange color persists for more than two to three days, then we might take action. The first thing we worry about is that your baby is not getting enough milk. This is most common in babies drinking breast milk. Your doctor may recommend getting a lactation consultant involved to help with breastfeeding. We also may need to address any medical conditions that might lead to decreased breast milk production in the mother.

If you see urate crystals at any time after your baby is five days old, it is a good idea to let your pediatrician know. Abnormalities in uric acid production or metabolism can lead to kidney stones that are made up of uric acid. Very rarely, the brick-colored urine of urate stones may be a precursor to uric acid kidney stones.

If your baby is a girl and the red color is coming from her vaginal area, then read the very next why question . . .

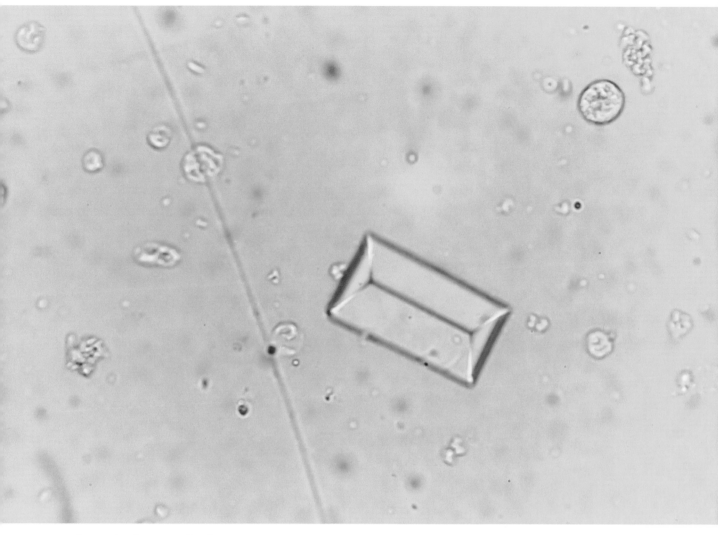

Istock.com/Todorean Gabriel

TAKE-HOME POINTS:

1. Orange-colored staining in the front of the diaper is usually caused by urate crystals.
2. It should happen when the baby is just a few days old and shouldn't last longer than three days.
3. If the orange color lasts longer than three days or happens any time after the newborn period, let your pediatrician know.
4. Calm down; it's very common the first few days of life and it is usually benign.

Why does my baby girl have mucus or blood in her vaginal area?

There are some things that we are just not prepared for when it comes to parenthood.

Okay, there are a *lot* of things we aren't prepared for when it comes to parenthood. When blood appears in places that you don't think it should be, most parents are going to freak out just a bit. This one is no exception. In fact, this one is a bit jolting. It's easy to understand. There has probably been nobody to warn you that your brand-new baby girl could be having blood or mucus come from her vaginal area. Well, it happens, and it's common.

Now you know it can happen, but why is it happening?

It all comes down to hormones. Mom is going to be painfully aware of hormones and periods. (Dad may be painfully aware of hormones as well, but for his personal safety it is best if he not mentions it.) Every month, different hormones surge that allow the miracle of pregnancy and birth to take place. Ladies, if you have ever used birth control pills you know that you take your hormone pill every day for usually 21 days and then you stop. About three days after you stop your pill, your period will begin. Some women do this to prevent pregnancy, but it has uses beyond that as well. Hormone therapy can be used to treat a variety of conditions.

In a baby, there are no pills or scheduled periods. Babies do get hormones, though.

Babies in utero are connected to their mom through their umbilical cord. As Mom's hormones surge with pregnancy, some of those hormones cross the placenta and go into the baby. At birth, the umbilical cord is cut and the flow of hormones from Mom stops. In the case of little girls, about three days later (notice the correlation), they can start to have a little mucus or light bloody discharge from their vaginal area. This is not going to be like menstrual flow-type blood. This will be more blood-tinged mucus and will just lightly stain the diaper. It's just enough blood to leave a small stain and induce a large panic.

It is nothing to worry about and will only last a couple of days. Just lightly wipe the area to remove it from the skin and don't give it a second thought. The only thing we as doctors worry about would be if it was lots of blood, it lasted longer than just two to three days, or if there was a foul discharge. If any of those were to happen, please contact your pediatrician. (I've been working with kids as a doctor for 22 years and it has never come up so far).

This is one of those why questions to which it's nice to know the answer beforehand so you can save yourself a ton of panic. (I hope you are reading this before it happens; if not, well, parenting, right?)

While we are talking about Mom's hormones and their effect on a baby, let's talk

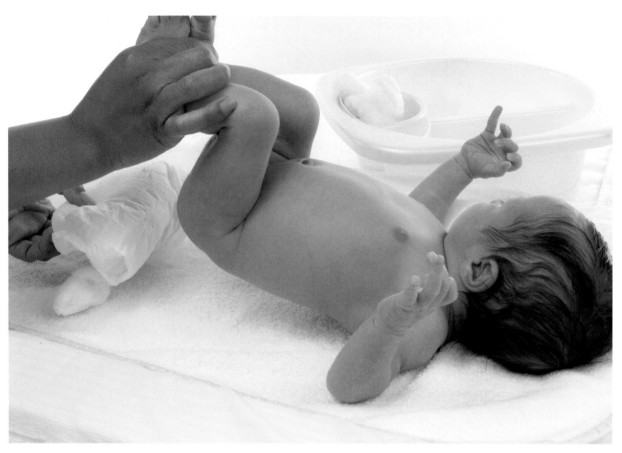

Istock.com/lostinbids

about breast buds. This can happen in both girls and boys. You may notice hard swelling under your baby's nipples. These are caused by maternal hormones and they will go away with time. In breastfed babies, they may last a bit longer due to the extended exposure to mom's hormones.

TAKE-HOME POINTS:

1. Blood or mucus from the vaginal area in a baby girl two to five days old is very common.
2. Just lightly clean the area; there is no need to scrub, which could hurt their delicate skin.
3. Don't freak out unless there is a ton of blood, it doesn't stop after three days, or if it has a smell.
4. Breast buds can happen in both girls and boys and are caused by exposure to maternal hormones.

Why does my baby boy's circumcision look infected?

Here is a topic that will get people excited. In fact, just in the last week I have seen two cases. In one such case, the parents had taken the baby to the emergency room without ever talking to me, only to be told what they thought was an issue was in fact completely normal.

By the way, don't do that! Your pediatrician is wonderful resource. Call them. I get calls all the time. If you need to go to the ER, we will send you there. Most times you do not.

In most cases, it isn't infected. Of course, there is a small possibility that it could be infected. Truth be told, it does *look* infected.

It's that slime. It's got the look of everything we generally consider an infection.

Let's take a moment and talk about circumcision. Most people think that a circumcision is just a little trimming of skin. It is a little more in-depth than just that. Your baby boy is born with skin that entirely covers the head of the penis. This is called foreskin. At the time of birth this foreskin is actually stuck to the skin on the head of the penis. In order to do a circumcision, the foreskin must be peeled away from the head of the penis. This causes a raw area that in the beginning looks like you peeled a cherry.

Istock.com/ Mladen Zivkovic

After the first day or so, a yellowish-green slime starts to cover the head of the penis. This yellow-green slime is part of the healing process and tends to look more like a burn healing than a scrape or cut. It tends to last for about three to five days after the circumcision.

Whew! Now that we know it isn't infected, is there anything else I need to know?

As a matter of fact, yes. It is important to keep some Vaseline or some sort of lubricant on the circumcision or the front of the diaper to keep the raw skin from sticking to the diaper. How long should you use the lubricant? I base it on the yellow slime. When the slime is all gone and the head of the penis doesn't look like it has any raw areas, then you are good to stop using it.

There are some things to watch for. Remember I said almost none of them have an infection? Here's when you do need to contact a doctor. If the head of the penis is swelling bigger than what it was right after the circumcision, that's a bad sign. Also, if you notice a foul smell, or if there is any heat or redness going down the shaft of the penis, that too is a sign of trouble. Definitely contact a doctor if a fever is present. Remember my rule from the chapter on fevers. A fever in a newborn is ALWAYS an emergency.

After the circumcision is completely healed and your baby is older than about 10 days, it is time to make sure you pull back on the foreskin until you see the rim around the edge of the head of the penis. As a baby boy starts to get a little chunkier, there is a fat pad right above the penis. This little fat pad can cause the foreskin to slide over the head of the penis. This is okay and normal, but if you don't gently pull back this skin with each diaper change, irritation can occur and the skin of the foreskin and the skin on the head of the penis can stick back together. This can then need to be corrected by your pediatrician and sometimes even necessitates a re-circumcision. You will need to pull back the foreskin until your baby is about 18 months or so. The fat pad usually goes away by then and they tend to do plenty of pulling on their own.

If you haven't been diligent in pulling back the skin on a regular basis, you may pull the skin back and notice some chalky, white material. This is not a sign of infection. This is old dead skin that has sloughed off, but had nowhere to go. We call this dead skin smegma. Simply wipe it off gently and don't give it a second thought.

TAKE-HOME POINTS:

1. A greenish-yellow slime on the head of the penis after circumcision is part of the normal healing process.
2. The slime will usually be gone within three to five days after the circumcision.
3. If you see any excessive swelling, foul smell, spreading redness, or fever contact your doctor.
4. Make sure once all the skin is healed up that you retract the foreskin off the head of the penis and clean it with each diaper change until your baby is about 18 months old.
5. A white-looking discharge or flaky skin is common around the head of the penis and is called smegma.

Why does my baby pause his breathing while asleep?

They say that confession is good for the soul. Well, I have something to confess. Even with all my training and knowledge, I still get a little freaked out by things that seem a little scary.

I was a pediatrician before I ever had a baby. When we brought my oldest home, I just loved to stare at him and hold him. I especially loved to watch him sleep. That said, he'd do something that would concern me. All of a sudden, he would start to have these pauses in his breathing. He would take a very deep breath, then he would have a pause that seemed to take forever, and then he'd take three to four very rapid breaths. As a pediatrician, I knew exactly what was going on, but as a parent I was scared.

If I was scared as a pediatrician, I can only imagine what it feels like to witness this event without the benefit of medical school. That memory is the reason I try to warn all my new parents about this the first time I see them. That memory is also the reason I have included this "Why" in the book.

Istock.com/Amax Photo

So, what is going on here?

This is called periodic breathing of the newborn. It is very common, thus the reason I warn every new parent I see. It is even more pronounced in premature infants. It is usually seen in periods of deep sleep, but it can happen in light sleep and sometimes even when they are awake. It is characterized by a pause of breathing for less than 10 seconds followed by three to five rapid breaths. The baby starts breathing on his own and needs no stimulation or help to continue breathing. The baby shouldn't be acting sick, have any color change, and or any vomiting.

The baby suffers no problems from this and will eventually outgrow it around the time he is three to six weeks old. The parents' side effects include gray hairs, heart palpitations, anxiety, and a lessening of expected lifespan.

Is there anything that we *should* worry about when our baby has pauses in his breathing? (Well of course there is, or I wouldn't have asked the question.) We worry if the pause lasts 20 seconds or longer, which is defined as apnea. Apnea can be a very subtle sign that your baby is getting sick, having problems with reflux, or even experiencing neurological problems.

There are certain times you should contact your doctor and have your baby seen. If your baby has any color change during these episodes, that's a red flag. If your baby vomits during or after these pauses, you should contact your pediatrician. Also look for problems breathing, a fever, or signs of difficulty rousing or waking. Don't confuse this normal occurrence with a real issue. If you have to make any interventions to make your baby start breathing, you need to see a doctor as soon as possible.

For most of us, these little pauses are just a part of life with a newborn. It's just a little pause in breathing followed by a little rapid breathing to catch up. If the whole event takes place over a few seconds and none of the bad symptoms I mentioned are present, everything is fine.

TAKE-HOME POINTS:

1. Periodic breathing of the newborn is very common the first several weeks and is characterized by a pause in breathing lasting less than 10 seconds and followed by three to five rapid breaths.
2. If the pause is over 20 seconds, you need to contact your doctor.
3. If the pause in breathing is associated with any of the following, contact your doctor immediately:
   - color change
   - difficulty breathing
   - fever
   - respiratory distress
   - vomiting
   - needing help to start breathing
4. Keep score on these little moments of terror. They come in handy down the road when your child is making fun of your gray hair, loss of hair, and wrinkles. It is always nice if you can blame it all on the child.

Why does my newborn sneeze so much?

I used to get this question all the time. It came as questions in visits, on Facebook, and even phone calls in the middle of the night. Finally, I got smart and just started answering the question before it got asked, during the very first office visit. (Now I am being even more preemptive and putting it in a book.) The day that a parent walks into my office for their child's first visit, and the baby sneezes and the parent tells me it's all right, they already know why, I may dance a little jig or something.

Istock.com/Artfoliophoto

Your newborn is sneezing so much because she needs to.

A sneeze is a way to open up the nasal passages. We have little nerves in our nose that let our nervous system know if there is something blocking our airway. The message goes in and a big ol' sneeze comes out. The sneeze is a violent exit of air through the nasal and oral passages and whatever was in the way has now been removed, hopefully.

What kinds of things get in the way? Well, since babies breathe mostly through their nose, the nasal passage acts as a filter to remove things from the air. These things include: dust, allergens, lint, and anything else that causes particles that we don't want or need in our lungs. Other things cause our nose to think it is plugged as well, such as: mucus, amniotic fluid in the case of a newborn, and even a finger touching a nerve when she is picking her nose.

There is one circumstance where you will see even more sneezing. This is when your baby is born by C-section. Remember how one of the things that could cause sneezing was amniotic fluid? Well, in the case of a C-section, the baby has more of that amniotic fluid to try and get out of the way. These babies will have little fits of sneezing, and it is completely normal.

Does a sneeze ever mean that they are sick? Only if it is accompanied by some other symptoms. If you are seeing a runny nose, cough, fussiness, or fever, then your baby is possibly sick. If your baby has a fever or is having a problem breathing, then you should talk to or see your doctor about those things. Sneezing itself isn't a reason to see your doctor. Only when the sneezing is bundled with other symptoms should you be alarmed.

The important thing to remember is that a sneeze is a perfectly normal thing for your baby to do and by itself is nothing to worry about. It needs to happen to keep the baby's airway open and free of debris. Since a baby can't really snort, sniff, or blow her nose, a sneeze is the only cleaning she can do to her nose. (Well, until she learns to stick her finger a couple of knuckles deep into it.)

TAKE-HOME POINTS:

1. Sneezing is a very normal and necessary thing for your baby to do.
2. Sneezing is just a form of maintenance to keep the nasal passages clean and clear.
3. Only worry about sneezing if it is accompanied by other symptoms like runny nose, cough, or fever.
4. Don't be surprised if your baby sneezes multiple times in a row. They will usually sneeze until they get their nose clear.

Why can't I give my baby water to drink?

This is one of those "gotcha" kind of questions. It's highly counter-intuitive. Water is a basic need for all of us, right? Well, not so fast. Babies have to get water to stay hydrated, this is true. They are on an all-liquid diet for the first few months. Whether it's breast milk or formula, both have a very high water content. This should be all the water they need. Unless your doctor directs you to do so, don't give them plain water to drink until about six months or so.

The question is still, why can't I give my baby just water?

The answer comes down to salt.

It is important to keep a baby's electrolytes properly balanced. Both formula and breast milk will have a good balance of electrolytes. Plain water has a near-zero electrolyte level. Giving a baby water can throw things out of balance by overloading his delicate system. The body tries to absorb the water but in doing so too much salt is flushed

Istock.com/rclassenlayouts

out. If the sodium level in his blood dips too low, it causes a condition called hyponatremia (medical lingo for low sodium). This can lead to swelling of the cells in the brain, which can make the baby very sick, lethargic, incur seizures, and even die.

Yes, there are babies who die every year from people either giving them water because they think they need more hydration or watering down breast milk or formula in order to make it last longer to save money. Please hear me on this—*never* water down breast milk, and *always* mix formula in the exact ratio indicated on the package.

It is important to know that a baby gets all the fluid it needs the first year through its milk, either breast milk or formula. Breast milk and formula have the exact amounts of electrolytes your baby needs on a daily basis to make everything work perfect. Again, breast milk is perfect as is. Formula must be mixed in the proper ratio, always.

A baby does not need "extra" water if he is hot, sweaty, sick, or just acting thirsty. If he needs more fluid only give it via their milk until they are at least six months old. Do not give him or her water unless your doctor is directing it and adhere strictly to how the doctor tells you to administer the water, in that case.

So, what happens at six months? At six months of age, a baby's kidneys mature and it is able to get rid of excess water that it doesn't need. With this comes the ability to regulate electrolytes. Nevertheless, even after six months, milk should be what a baby drinks most of the time.

Hopefully I have convinced you at this point, and baby will not be getting any water. In case you are curious, there are other issues water can cause. Water will fill them up and not allow them to get the proper amount of nutrients they obtain via their milk. Their little tummies only have so much room. Water can also cause problems with absorption in babies. Water by itself is very difficult to absorb by infants, so it can lead to abdominal pain and nausea.

TAKE-HOME POINTS:

1. Don't give your baby anything to drink except breast milk or formula until they are six months of age. Even after six months, milk should be what they drink most of the time.
2. Water by itself can make your baby sick by lowering their sodium level. This low level can cause hyponatremia, which can make your baby sick, lethargic, cause them pain, and lead to seizures and even death in extreme cases.
3. Make sure you give breast milk or formula in full strength. Do not dilute to make it last longer.
4. Never give anything other than full-strength formula or breast milk to your baby unless under direct guidance from your pediatrician.

Why are my baby's eyes funny colored?

I don't know if anybody has ever asked me why their baby's eyes are funny colored, but I have had tons of questions about the color of their eyes. When the baby is first born, the most common question from parents is often, what color are my baby's eyes? The follow-up question is then, what color do you think my baby's eyes will be? Finally, I will get the question of, when will my baby's eye color be permanent? This is one of the fun questions in pediatrics and I love to talk about it.

I like to describe a newborn's eye color as "muck." I'm not sure what color in the crayon box you could pull out and get it to match their eye color. They look more like you gave your three-year-old some finger paint and they decided to mix them all up together and invent a new color. It's not a good color, it's not a pretty color, and it definitely isn't a color that you recognize. I call it muck and it's the color your baby's eyes pretty much start out looking like. There are different varieties of "muck," which is why I like it as a definition. It is much more fluid than pinning us down to one colored crayon.

Over the first several months of life, your baby will start to have an eye color that resembles something you may be able to identify. I tell parents all the time, "Don't get too attached to their eye color, it can change." Pediatricians usually agree that permanent eye color is achieved somewhere between

Istock.com/bulentumut

nine to twelve months of age. The change we usually see after nine months is usually pretty subtle, but it can still change a little.

The cause of eye color is melanin. Melanin is the substance in our skin that gives it color. If you have dark skin you have more melanin, whereas if you have light-colored skin you have less melanin. Our skin secretes more melanin when we get tan. Melanin in the front part of the eye is what determines eye color. Lots of melanin and your eyes will be very dark. Very little melanin and your eyes will be blue. Somewhere in the middle and you will end up with green or hazel eyes.

Eye color is usually determined by genetics. The eye color of your parents and their parents have a great impact on your eye color, which is equally determined by both sets of parents. Brown eyes are dominant and blue eyes are recessive, so we end up with more brown-eyed babies than we do blue ones. Most of the time, if you have two blue-eyed parents you will end up with a blue-eyed baby. If you have brown-eyed parents you can have a baby with brown eyes, hazel eyes, green eyes, or blue. Very rarely a set of blue-eyed parents can have a brown-eyed baby, but that is usually a fluke caused by a broken gene in one of the parents that led them to have blue eyes when genetically their eyes should have been brown. Trust me when I say that the genetics of eye color is way more complicated than we want to go into in this book.

Sometimes babies can have two different colored eyes. It is called congenital heterochromia when it is present since infancy and is usually benign. If it happens when a person is older, it is often caused by some disease or trauma. If your baby has two different eye colors, it isn't a bad idea to mention it to your doctor to make sure there isn't anything to worry about. I always refer them to ophthalmology just to make sure.

So, there you have it! That eye color they are born with is mostly a blue/grey that will change as more melanin gets deposited in the front part of the eye. More melanin indicates darker colored eyes. For the most part your parents' and grandparents' genes will be determining your eye color, but occasionally there is a break in the system and you can end up with eyes that are not determined by genetics at all.

TAKE-HOME POINTS:

1. The eye color your baby is born with is probably not their permanent eye color.
2. In most cases, eye color will be permanent by the time your baby is nine to twelve months of age.
3. Just because the eye color of your baby doesn't match the parents' doesn't mean any hanky-panky happened.
4. If your baby has eyes that are two different colors or change after they are a year old, it is a good idea to talk to your doctor.

Why shouldn't I use baby powder on my baby?

In truth, this should be a different question. It should be why would you ever want to use baby powder on your baby? I know it sounds silly to denounce something as seemingly innocuous as talcum powder/baby powder. There is some very solid science behind it though.

Baby powder, or talcum powder, has a long history of use to keep babies dry. It absorbs moisture and was previously thought to be very safe. It is also very cheap and readily available.

If you're old enough to be a parent, chances are you had talcum powder on your butt.

Yet as time passed, scientists started noticing some problems. Some babies were experiencing respiratory problems. Chronic cough and wheezing were noted in conjunction with baby powder use. It was also noticed that the miners who worked in talc mines were having chronic breathing problems.

For one moment, I am hopping on my soapbox. Please, whether you're in a work

environment where you breathe particles, or you are a hobby woodworker, or whatever. Please, please wear protection. Your lungs are hard to fix once polluted. Protect them.

The talcum powder particles are so tiny that they can get into the deepest parts of the lung when inhaled. In the case of babies, these little talc particles were then causing inflammation that was leading to lung disease or chronic cough.

Sadly, this isn't the worst of it.

In the 1980s it was found that talcum powder applied near the vaginal area was causing an increase in ovarian cancer. In fact, there have been multimillion-dollar lawsuits won against some of the giant baby powder producers due to the link between talcum powder and ovarian cancer.

The link between ovarian cancer and talcum powder is very real, but they are not exactly sure why. Asbestos and talcum are often mined in the same area. Cross-contamination could be the culprit. Perhaps talcum itself is to blame; possibly it irritates the delicate skin in the ovaries the way it does the lungs? Science is unsure of the cause, but it is certain that talcum powder is not safe for ovaries.

Due to this overwhelming evidence, pediatricians have taken it upon themselves to try and get parents to stop using baby powder. There are multiple safe ways to treat diaper rash. There is no good reason to risk using baby powder. Initially it was just warned to not use the powder near the baby; now we just tell parents to not use baby powder at all.

You'd think with all this at risk, the stuff would be out of use completely. One would assume that a bottle of talcum powder would come with a huge warning label like on a pack of cigarettes.

Right? Well, yeah. One would *think* that. Unfortunately, that's not the reality.

Here is the problem. Baby powder has been used forever! Baby powder was introduced before the turn of the century in the late 1800s. From then until now, it has graced a lot of baby butts. It is difficult to get people to stop doing something that has been commonly used for that long. When your mom, her mom, and her mom's mom all used it . . . you get the idea.

Many things that pediatricians try to warn against doing still get done on a daily basis because it goes against the mom and grandma advice. Your mom and grandma mean well. If they bring it up, educate them. Educate your friends. I do again acknowledge this seems a little silly to get so adamant about. My hope is that knowing the risks will enable you to take the dangers seriously.

TAKE-HOME POINTS:

1. Don't use baby powder near your baby.
2. Don't use baby powder on your baby.
3. Don't use baby powder.
4. Seriously. Just don't.
5. Lung disease, chronic cough, and in girls the potential of ovarian cancer are reasons to stay away.

Why does my baby get hiccups?

This is one of the questions that every parent will ask. That should tell you something right there. If every parent is asking about hiccups, that would mean . . . every baby gets hiccups. That should also tell you that they are normal and nothing to worry about. Unfortunately, that will not help you because as parents we tend to worry about everything. Every baby cries, poops, etc. and it didn't stop us from worrying about it, now did it?

What is a hiccup? The actual sound of a hiccup is made by our epiglottis slamming shut. If you are not familiar with what the epiglottis is, it is a flap that automatically covers the trachea (windpipe) whenever we are swallowing. Its job is to keep fluid or food from going down the trachea and into the lungs. The cause of the hiccup is a spasm of the diaphragm. Your diaphragm is a muscle between the lungs and the intestine that regulates breathing.

Why does the diaphragm go into spasm? Good question! In short, we don't know. No one has the exact answer as to why it happens. We do have a bunch of theories and I will let you know some of them.

You probably noticed your baby having hiccups before it was even born. It is thought that this is a normal maturation process that is preparing the baby to be able to breathe once it is born. There is also the theory that the baby is practicing swallowing and when she swallows hard it will cause the diaphragm to spasm. The take-home is that it is normal and something she "needs" to do.

After the baby is born, we know that she is more likely to have hiccups when she is very young and as she gets older, she tends to have fewer hiccups. As adults, we are bothered by hiccups even though they cause no real pain. We then think that since it bothers us, it must bother the baby as well. For the most part, they seem to be unfazed by the hiccups and sometimes even seem to find them amusing. There is the occasional baby that seems to be upset by the hiccups, but that is most likely thinking of the problem backwards. The actual story is something is bothering the baby and it is causing hiccups.

There are babies that seem to have hiccups a lot more than just the normal baby. Is there anything that you need to worry or think about? Babies that swallow very hard will oftentimes cause themselves to have hiccups. This can be caused by bottle nipples that are flowing faster than the baby can handle. It can also be a sign that the baby is filling their mouth too full before actually swallowing. The nipple size we can fix, but the greedy baby is something she will have to learn on her own. We also know that babies who have reflux (where milk or stomach contents are coming back up into the mouth) have more hiccups. This is something that you need to talk to your doctor about. The hiccups by themselves aren't a reason to treat reflux, but your doctor should know and ask more questions to determine if anything needs to be done.

Istock.com/szefei

Rarely, a seizure can cause hiccups. Just like a seizure can cause body parts to shake, a seizure can cause the muscle of the diaphragm to go into spasm. If you see that your baby is acting odd or getting very sleepy after having a bout of hiccups, let your doctor know. Do remember that this is very rare and not a common cause of hiccups at all.

You will hear a ton of old wives' tales on how to cure hiccups. Most of them have been found to be pretty ineffective. Some are completely harmless. Trying to scare or surprise your baby probably isn't going to hurt them, but they won't like it. Giving them something to drink may help as well. I have heard every possible combination of gulping or sipping something that is warm or cold. It won't cause any harm as long as you are just giving your baby their normal milk, and it might help. Never do anything that could hurt your baby like pounding on their back too hard or submersing their head in water. The hiccups will go away on their own, and most of the time they are bothering you more than they are bothering your baby.

TAKE-HOME POINTS:

1. Hiccups are completely normal.
2. Hiccups are most likely needed in the maturation process of the lungs and intestinal tract.
3. You need to talk to your doctor if the hiccups go on for longer than 30 minutes, if your baby is spitting up often, or if your baby is acting odd and falls asleep after having the hiccups.

Why did my baby become jaundiced?

I am going to start off with an apology to anyone who happens to be a gastroenterologist, neonatologist, or student of physiology. If any of those labels apply to you, you might want to just turn the page now. I am going to greatly oversimplify this so the person without your training can understand the big picture on this issue. I cannot be held responsible for any emotional outbursts on your part going forward.

I'm sure you could write a very lengthy book just covering the topic of jaundice. The problem would be the average person couldn't understand most of it. In addition, it would be so boring no one would read it. There's nothing terribly exciting about discussing jaundice.

My goal with this question is to make you adequately informed to understand the basics of what is going on. If you want more in-depth understanding, I am sure there's a

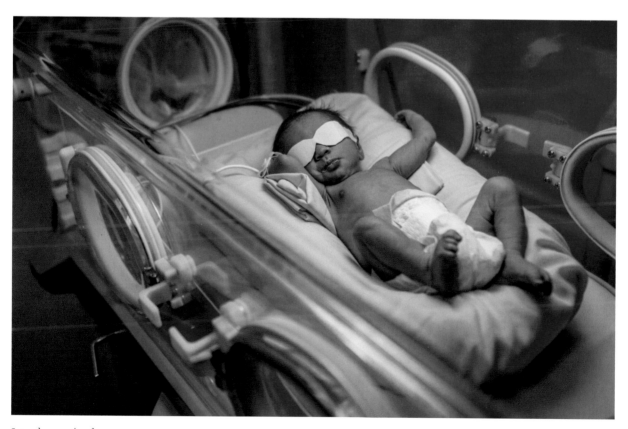

Istock.com/andresr

gastroenterologist out there willing to sell you their old textbook on it.

First up, what is jaundice?

Jaundice is the term that describes your skin, eyes, and mucous membranes (like the skin inside your mouth) turning yellow, orange, or green. It is caused by an elevated level of bilirubin.

Bilirubin is a breakdown product from old red blood cells.

There are several things that combine to make your baby look jaundiced. First, a fetus has a higher red blood count than a born human. They need this in order to steal oxygen from their mother while in utero. After a baby is born and they breathe on their own, the need for the elevated red blood cell count is lost, so the body begins eliminating the excess. In the process of breaking down all those red blood cells, their bilirubin level goes up.

The way that we naturally get rid of bilirubin is through our stool and our urine (mostly stool). When a baby is first born, the first stools they pass are called meconium and don't help them eliminate bilirubin. It is only when the stools turn yellow and green that the baby is actively getting rid of bilirubin. If stools stay too long in the intestine, the baby's body will actually reabsorb the bilirubin and she has to try again to get rid of it.

Babies aren't eating very much the first several days and for breastfed babies they are eating even less. So, a baby isn't pooping as much as she needs to eliminate the bilirubin and it starts to build up and turn their skin a yellowish-green or orange color. As the level gets higher, more of the baby's body looks yellow and it gets brighter in color.

Bilirubin levels usually peak between days three and five of life. Babies that are breastfed tend to have higher levels due to decreased amounts of breast milk to drink and therefore less elimination through stool. Babies with lighter-colored skin tend to look more jaundiced, but don't actually have higher levels.

Why do we care if the baby is yellow?

It isn't the color of their skin that we are worried about. We are worried about the bilirubin level getting high enough that it enters the brain and causes damage. This entry of bilirubin into the brain is called kernicterus. Kernicterus can lead to the baby having symptoms of poor feeding, poor muscle tone, and more fatigue. Long-term, it can lead to problems with seizures, mental retardation, hearing problems, muscle problems, and even problems with eye movements. These problems are preventable by recognizing jaundice early and treating the baby to prevent kernicterus.

If your baby is recognized to have jaundice, your doctor may order a couple of different tests. One common test is usually performed at the hospital in the nursery. There is a small tool that detects the level of bilirubin through the skin. If the levels look significantly elevated, then the doctor will order a blood test to get a more accurate bilirubin level. The level of concern varies with factors like age and weight. Causes of concern like prematurity or issues causing premature destruction of red blood cells will factor in as well.

The treatment for most babies is going to be phototherapy. Remember up above when we said that the main ways to get rid of bilirubin is via stool and urine? Phototherapy is a way to convert the bilirubin that has deposited in the skin into a form that can be actively eliminated via the urine. This allows for a speedier process. During phototherapy, babies are encouraged to eat more so that they will also increase their stooling.

You may hear that it helps to place your baby in sunlight to lower the baby's bilirubin. I know I have been pretty hard on folk wisdom in this book, but this one has some truth to it. In fact, this is how phototherapy came to be. Doctors discovered that babies lying next to the windows with direct sunlight had fewer problems with jaundice. They were right. The blue-green wavelength of light will help with bilirubin elimination.

It is, however, not a good practice today for a couple of reasons. The main issue is that we have different types of windows. Our modern windows now filter out different wavelengths of light. The blue-green light that is needed to convert bilirubin to a water-soluble form is largely eliminated as it passes through our modern glass windows. Additionally, we have phototherapy lights that produce the exact spectrum needed to help with bilirubin elimination, and they are far more effective than the old method of putting the crib near a window. Finally, as covered in another "Why" in this book, exposing a very young baby to direct sunlight opens a Pandora's box to a host of other issues.

There are other more extreme ways to reduce levels of bilirubin that are only used in extremely severe and special conditions. These involve exchange transfusions and are only done in intensive care units. These cases are extremely rare and very serious.

Today, thanks to awareness, we very rarely have any babies that suffer from kernicterus. Your doctor should be screening for jaundice in the newborn period and will be testing as needed. If there is an issue, in most cases phototherapy will solve the problem and eliminate the elevated bilirubin. Always, *always* talk to your doctor if your baby seems to have jaundice.

TAKE-HOME POINTS:

1. It is very common for your baby to look a little yellow the first several days of life.
2. Bilirubin and therefore jaundice usually peaks at days three to five of life.
3. Doctors are trained to look and assess for jaundice in the newborn period, but if your baby is looking yellow to you, always ask your doctor.
4. Kernicterus is irreversible brain damage caused by elevated bilirubin levels and is completely preventable by proper diagnosis and treatment of jaundice.

Why do babies need a car seat?

When I was a kid, we didn't have car seats. In fact, I remember some of our cars not having seat belts. My parents never wore seat belts and we were fine. Why should we use car seats now? They say that cars are much safer than they were back then, right? We even have laws that make the roads safer.

Here is an example of logic that isn't logic at all. It was true that we did not have a car seat when I was little and nobody was wearing a seat belt, but we also were never in a wreck. By never being in a wreck, we never had to test out that lack of safety we were exercising. If we had been in a wreck, you likely wouldn't be reading this right now.

The problem was that there were wrecks then and we have the statistics to show that the number of childhood deaths due to car accidents in the mid-'70s was over twice what it is today. Keep in mind there are more cars on the road today, which technically increases your risk of having a wreck. The use of seat belts and car seats has dramatically changed the chance of surviving a car accident.

It is even more important for a baby to use a car seat, because they are so much more likely to be harmed in an accident. I tell people all the time that babies are tougher than we give them credit for, but they have some vulnerabilities that can get them hurt in a car accident.

First, they aren't paying attention. They are going to have absolutely no warning that a car accident is about to happen. As an adult, you might see a crash coming. You will instinctively tense up and brace for impact. You will probably raise your arms in front of your face as a reflex. Kids, especially babies, don't do any of this. If left to their own devices they are going to be moving around, in awkward angles and in more dangerous places in the car. I remember being a little kid and lying in the back window of the car as we drove along. I was just asking to become a flying projectile.

Second, especially in a very young baby, they lack muscle tone. This means that they are floppier and things like their very large heads can easily be thrown back and forth violently. Accidents usually come with sudden stops, turns, or even flipping over. Just because an arm or a seat in front of a baby stopped his body from going forward at a great rate of speed, it doesn't mean that his head is going to stop at the same time. This can lead to severe damage to the neck and spine.

Third, a baby has a very soft little head until about a year old. The bones in the skull are not fused together. This is an important thing that allows a baby to fit through the birth canal. It also allows for rapid growth of the baby's brain. On the flip side, it poses a serious risk when hit in the head with high forces.

Finally, I remember not having car seats when I was little. I have no idea how my dad paid attention to the road. We were all over the place. We were flipping over the seats, wrestling in the back seats, climbing around on the floor, and fighting for space. Car seats keep kiddos

Istock.com/herjua

still and in one spot and decrease the distraction of the driver. Why is this story even necessary? Well, for one it shows how far we have come in the protection of our babies, but still to this day I will have grandparents question the need for car seats, because they didn't use them.

So, we got it settled that your baby needs a car seat. Now what?

Now we have to decide on what type of car seat. A baby, until they are at least two, needs to have a rear-facing car seat. This is the law in several states already, and it will become the law in all of them eventually. It just makes sense to protect a baby's head and neck when their head and neck are the most vulnerable. Some babies will hate it; some of them will scream and cry and kick and act like they are dying. No amount of noise that

they make will equal the anguish you will experience if you didn't protect them to the best of your abilities and they got hurt. They will also scream and cry and act like they are dying when you don't let them stick a pair of scissors in an electrical outlet . . . so put it in the same category.

When buying a car seat, do your research. Look online for reviews, look for history of a company having recalls, look at articles that have side-by-side comparisons. More expensive doesn't always equal better; sometimes it is just trying to be a fashion accessory. You want the safest car seat that you can buy. (I am not even going to try and point you in a direction because they are always changing. There is a good chance there will be a new line with new advancements or problems before this book even gets to print.) Just do your research, make the best decision you can at the time, and feel comfortable in that decision.

Never buy a used car seat for your baby. You do not know what has happened with it. Car seats that have been in an accident need to be thrown away. There are parts of it that are meant to absorb impact once. After that, you can't trust it. You have probably heard about not dropping a helmet, right? They tell you if you drop a helmet from more than a foot or so, throw it out. The same principle applies here. Also, exposure to sunlight and extremes in temperature can weaken plastic. Car seats have an expiration date for that reason. Just be safe! Always buy your own car seat so that you know you are starting off as safe as you possibly can.

Get someone to check out the installation of your car seat. Fire departments are a wonderful resource for this. Stop by your local fire department; they are happy to help you install the seat properly. There is a good chance you have done it wrong. Don't feel dumb or guilty. Some estimate that up to 60 percent are installed incorrectly. (I would have been one of them with my first child and I was already a pediatrician.)

After two years of age or when the child outgrows his rear-facing car seat you will want to go to a forward-facing car seat that continues to have a four-point restraint. If you have a convertible car seat you may not be changing seats, but you will be changing positioning. Again, when you change car seats, go get the installation checked for safety. Vehicles newer than 2002 or so should have the LATCH system for car seats. The LATCH system is easier to use than seat belts, and very secure.

A lot of fire stations, police stations, and hospitals have people that will install or check your installation for free. It is well worth your investment in time to be extra safe and even relieve some of the frustration you will have in installing the car seat. Whether using the LATCH system or seat belts, they can help.

Check on your individual state laws and the ever-changing recommendations on how long a child should be in a car seat. At this time, it is at least until they are four and they get to the height that the seat belt goes across their shoulder and not their neck to go into a booster seat. They will then be in the booster until they are at least nine. Again, check your individual state laws and the American Academy of Pediatrics recommendations as to when it is safe for them to just use a seat belt. Most laws now are they need to be about nine, but the AAP recommends it until they are twelve years old, or four foot nine inches tall.

TAKE-HOME POINTS:

1. Your baby and child need a car seat. Don't let anybody convince you that they don't.
2. They should be in a rear-facing car seat until at least two years old, a forward-facing car seat until at least four years old, and a booster seat until they are twelve or at least four foot nine inches tall.
3. Get the installation of your baby's car seat checked by a professional.
4. Always be aware of recalls. If your car seat isn't safe, get a new one.

Why do doctors worry so much about fevers in a baby less than two months old?

The answer would be meningitis, urinary tract infections, and sepsis. Throwing out a bunch of big-city medical school words isn't "Why" you bought this book though, is it? Let's dig a little deeper.

Very young babies don't have a very strong immune system. After all, it's brand-new. This causes two problems.

First, the baby doesn't have a great defense system to fight off severe infections. Most of us know the basics of the immune system. Your body gets exposed to things, learns to fight those things, and retains the knowledge for future infections. Obviously, it is *a lot* more complex than that, but you get the gist of it. Your baby hasn't been exposed to much of anything yet and therefore has very little resistance to infections.

Second, the baby doesn't show much as far as symptoms when they are severely ill. So again, without being too simplistic...a lot of what we regard as "symptoms" are actually

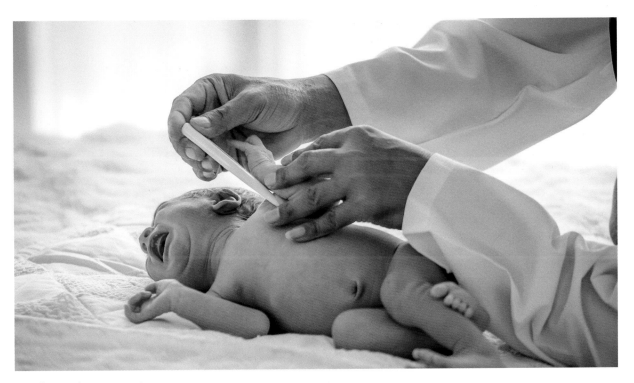

Istock.com/Narongrit Sritana

immunological response to an infection. A fever, for instance. A fever is your body raising your temp to make you an unhospitable environment for whatever bug you have. Making it sound this simple is bound to get me some hate mail from virologists, so suffice to say all of this is much, much more complex than I am describing. We just don't need to get into the nitty-gritty details for the purposes of this question.

So, we have a small human that has a very limited ability to respond to hostile infections, and when they do respond, their limited response makes it so we have little in the way of symptoms to help us diagnose the issue.

Because of that, we need to be very suspicious of any sign of infection. We set the limit of a temperature above 100.4°F. Depending on how conservative your pediatrician is, they will ring the panic bell if your child is less than one or two months old. The less conservative pediatricians draw the line at one month of age because at that time the baby develops a blood-brain barrier. That means there is a defense mechanism that prevents bacteria that might be in the blood from entering into the brain. The more conservative pediatrician draws the line at two months when the baby gets his first set of vaccines.

If your newborn, less than two months of age, gets a temp over 100.4°F, we as pediatricians want to see your baby *now*! We want to look your baby over to see if we can find the source of the fever. If a reason is not found on exam, we will order blood work, urine tests, and usually even do a lumbar puncture to make sure your baby does not have a severe infection. It is not unusual for these babies to spend a day or two in the hospital just to make sure they are not severely ill.

It is for this reason that I am very conservative with my own patients and tell my parents to avoid crowded places like busy stores in peak hours, churches, and schools. It is very traumatic for the baby and the family to be in the hospital, so I like to avoid it as much as possible.

TAKE-HOME POINTS:

1. Fevers can sometimes be the only sign of a serious infection in a small baby.
2. How high the fever is won't necessarily directly coincide with how sick your baby is. A low-grade fever of 100.4°F could be the only sign a baby has of a serious illness.
3. A fever above 100.4°F is considered an emergency in a newborn.
4. An ounce of prevention is worth a pound of cure: avoid exposing your baby to unnecessary germs by avoiding crowds of people in the first two months of life.

Why do I have to burp my baby?

The simple answer is so they don't get a belly-ache and cry. Okay, fair enough. So, they don't cry *as much*.

The correct answer would be because they need a little help in the beginning. They're new to this whole being human thing, and you're their guide. Even simple things like burping that we take for granted are a new experience for them.

Babies swallow a lot of air. Mostly it happens when they are crying and while they are eating. Once the air is in their intestinal tract, it has to come out one end or the other. If they don't burp, it will continue through their stomach, small intestines, large intestines, and eventually out in the form of flatulence (passing gas, a toot, a poot, a fart, or as my wife was taught when she was a little girl, a pixie).

So, what happens if they don't burp? Then they will pass gas and that's that. Problem solved. The issue is in the middle between the swallowing of air and the passing of gas it may give them gas pain, which can lead

Istock.com/DGLimages

to some crying and screaming fits. Babies, of course, have one main method of communication, so they will continue to cry and scream until the gas pain subsides.

As parents, we would like to avoid the screaming for our own sanity, but we would also like to save our baby some suffering. It's important to remember this. It's easy to get stressed by a loudly agitated baby. Maybe all they need is a little help with a burp or waiting for things to pass out the other end. They will not explode; it will be fine. Well, *they'll* be fine. You may need a moment after a good crying fit. Hold them, comfort them; this too will … pass.

Some babies will be easy to burp, and others like to make you work at it. The process of burping includes holding your child upright—this is so the air goes to the top of the stomach and closer to where the esophagus (passageway from mouth to stomach) meets the stomach. The patting, rubbing, and bouncing are trying to get all the air bubbles to join together as well as relaxing the baby so he will let a burp come out.

PLEASE NOTE: Patting harder will not help your baby to burp faster or easier! This is dangerous, so don't do it!

TAKE-HOME POINTS:

1. We burp our babies to help them so they will not get a bellyache.
2. If they don't burp it is okay; the worst thing that will happen is they get a bellyache.
3. Somewhere between two and four months, they start to get where they swallow less air and can burp on their own, which means we get to stop burping them.
4. If at first you don't succeed, just keep trying. Try different positions and different ways to calm your baby. If patting isn't working, try bouncing around a bit. Sit in a rocking chair.
5. Mix a few movements together. Every baby is a little different and may respond better to different methods.
6. If you don't get a burp after trying for a while, it is okay. They will not explode, and sometimes they just don't need to burp!

Why can't I give my newborn a real bath?

It's a common question we pediatricians get. By the way, if you haven't heard not to give your newborn a bath, then let me be the first to tell you. Do not give your newborn a bath!

But ... why?

I agree it's a little counterintuitive. You likely just want to keep your baby happy, healthy, and clean. It's a noble pursuit, for sure. Most parents will recall that the nurses in the hospital gave the baby a bath; so, why can't we do it at home?

It speaks to the process of birth itself. Birth is wonderful, exciting. There's so much expectation and joy. It's a glorious process filled with glee and ... well ... bodily fluids. Let's face it; it's not very clean. In fact, it's downright messy. Perhaps it's Mother Nature's way of preparing you to be the parent of a toddler? It's a sound theory.

That bath in the hospital is pretty important. We need to get all the blood and bacteria off your baby's skin. It's presumably been a

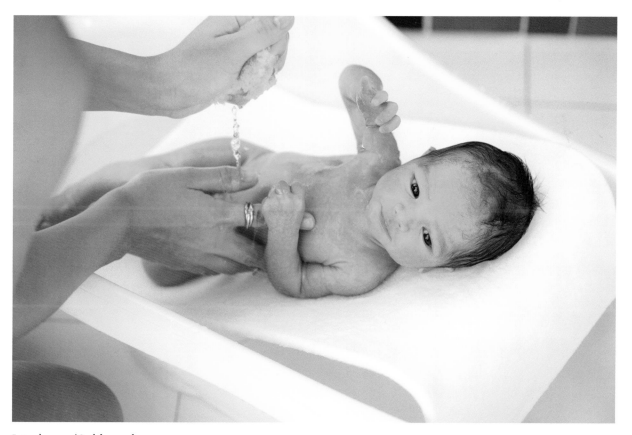

Istock.com/Goldmund

75

long day for both of you, and you both need to clean up a bit. Your baby is going to be touched by other people. It is best if the baby is still not covered in blood, amniotic fluid, stool, or urine when meeting the general public.

After that first bath, we recommend you only do sponge baths for the next couple of weeks or so. It should be more than enough to clean up the little messes that a newborn makes.

But still, *why*?

There are a few reasons why we don't want you giving your newborn baby a bath.

The first is the umbilical cord. That crusty little drying stump needs to stay dry and keep getting drier in order for it to fall off on schedule. Getting it wet not only will delay the process but can also increase the chances of it getting infected. Infections in a baby are a very serious thing, and anything that puts them at risk of one is not a good idea.

The second reason is that babies lose a lot of heat through their skin. They don't have great control of their temperatures yet. Getting them wet can cool them rapidly through evaporation. When their temp drops, they have to burn more calories to heat back up. Calories and growth are vital at this stage. We want them using those calories to get their birth weight back, not for heat.

The third reason is that a baby's skin is very dry. They will pretty much peel off the top layer of skin they were born with. Bathing them makes their skin even drier and will accelerate the peeling. This could lead to severe cracking of the skin, especially at the wrists and ankles. This can happen anyway, but bathing can make it worse.

The fourth reason is that they really don't need baths very often. They aren't crawling on the floor or rolling in dirt (that comes later, and sooner than you think). A simple sponge bath on the areas that have gotten dirty is more than enough for your newborn.

Now you know why we don't give our newborn a bath, so at what point can you give them a bath and how often?

You can give them a full submersed bath when:

1. They have lost their umbilical cord.
2. They have gotten back to their birth weight.
3. You have developed nerves of steel. No, I'm serious about this point. Giving your baby a bath is not nearly as fun as it looks like it is going to be. They are going to be wet and very slippery and you will feel like you are going to drown them. They are going to be very mad because they do not like being wet, cold, or naked, and you are doing all three to them at the same time. You will need to have many things ready to make this work without a hitch. Inevitably, you will forget something and you will be forced to make do while saving a near-drowning baby who is screaming at you. Oh, and the wiggling—the wiggle is real. So, there you are, with a slippery, wet, agitated, gyrating, fragile bundle of pure joy. All of this happens at a rate of speed that seems to defy logic, all while you are trying not to drop the slippery little baby on the floor.

TAKE-HOME POINTS:

1. Most people will tend to over-bathe their baby. They only need one or two baths a week until they start truly getting dirty. This will happen when they start moving around more and spending more time on the ground.

2. By bathing your baby too frequently, you will cause more bad than good. Bathing them too much dries out their skin.

3. Trust me, you will have years to fight with your child about taking a bath. Perhaps even into young adulthood. Treasure this magical time when they truly don't need one so often.

4. When it come to giving a baby a bath, preparation is key. Make sure you have everything you need pulled out before the bath. You will need your soap, a wash cloth, and a towel right beside the tub. You will then need clothes, a diaper, and any ointments or lotions that you're going to use already laid out.

Why did my baby come out with black and blue spots?

I know that birth can't be easy, but why did my baby come out looking like he lost a fight?

There can be several reasons that your baby could have black and blue spots on his skin. The first reason would be the one that generally comes to mind when you see black and blue spots . . . it could be bruises. Birth is traumatic for both mom and baby. Just ask mom while she is giving birth. (On second thought, don't do that. Ever. Don't ever, ever, *ever* do that.)

Sometimes, babies will have bruises due to the trauma of birth. The most common place to see bruising is on the top of their scalp. There may be bruising on the nose, the sides of the face, or the shoulders. In the case of breech presentations, their bottoms may get bruised. Sometimes the bruises are caused by the doctor helping with the delivery. Babies will sometimes get stuck and need to be pulled on to get out; this happens usually if a shoulder gets stuck. In the case of a suction-assisted delivery, the suction cup may leave a bruise. In extreme cases, a baby may need help with forceps to aid with delivery and the metal forceps could leave a bruise. It's tough being born!

Most parents asking me about the black and purple spots on their baby don't ask questions about how it happened. Most of the time when a baby has a bruise, the mommy is well aware of how they earned it. Chances are she is feeling like she went through the same fight and bruising is the least painful thing that happened.

The most common reason why parents are going to ask me about black and blue spots on their baby is because of a birthmark called a cerulean spot. Now before you start getting upset at the medical profession for its crazy way of naming things, cerulean is the name of an actual color. The color

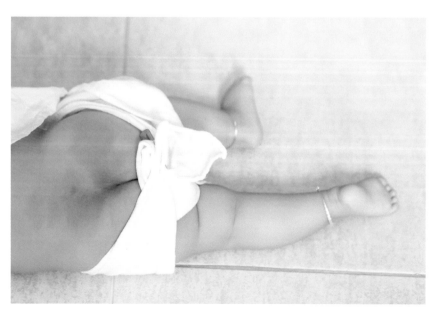

Istock.com/Pradit_Ph

is kind of a dark-blackish blue. These spots used to be called Mongolian spots, but that has been dropped from use due to the racist connotations.

A cerulean spot is a birthmark that is present at birth and is most frequently found on the back, buttocks, abdomen, and legs. It is seen more commonly in people from African, American Indian, Hispanic, Asian, and East Indian decent. Before you get too caught up in the racial differentiations, my youngest son had one at birth and he is as white as the driven snow. There is a racial predominance, but I have personally seen them on babies of all races. Cerulean spots are a collection of melanocytes in the skin. (This answer sure has a lot of big fancy words, huh? Maybe someday you'll be doing a crossword and you can thank me.) Melanocytes are what cause the pigment level in your skin color. In cerulean spots, there are just too many melanocytes, too close together.

Cerulean spots are not thought to have any complications associated with them. They do not lead to cancer and are not really indicative of any type of disease. They usually fade with age. In most cases, they will be gone by the time your child is a teenager. If they are on the face or they cause any type of mental trauma due to their existence, they can be removed or lightened with laser therapy by a dermatologist or plastic surgeon.

Is there anything that you need to worry about if your child has a cerulean spot?

Yes! You need to make sure that anyone taking care of your child knows that they have a cerulean spot on them and what they are. These spots are black and blue. They look like bruises. Imagine being the daycare worker caring for a new baby. You go to change the baby's diaper, and their little bottom is covered in black and blue splotches. You could easily think these are bruises. By law, any healthcare worker, school employee, or daycare worker who suspects child abuse must report it.

In my career I have had two families investigated for child abuse due to their child's cerulean spots. It's an awful thing to go through. Just point it out to them and you should be saved an embarrassing and scary investigation.

TAKE-HOME POINTS:

1. Black and blue spots on your baby are common and are either bruises from birth trauma and will fade fairly quickly after birth, or comprise a birthmark called a cerulean spot.
2. Cerulean spots are collections of pigment that cause the skin to look like a bruise.
3. Cerulean spots fade with age and do not require any treatment.
4. Make sure anyone watching your child knows that your child has a cerulean spot and educate that person about it.
5. If cerulean spots are cosmetically troubling, they can be lightened with laser therapy by a dermatologist or plastic surgeon.

PART 3
THE FIRST MONTH

"No one is ever quite ready; everyone is always caught off guard. Parenthood chooses you. And you open your eyes, look at what you've got, say 'Oh, my gosh,' and recognize that of all the balls there ever were, this is the one you should not drop. It's not a question of choice."

——Marisa de los Santos, author of *Love Walked In*

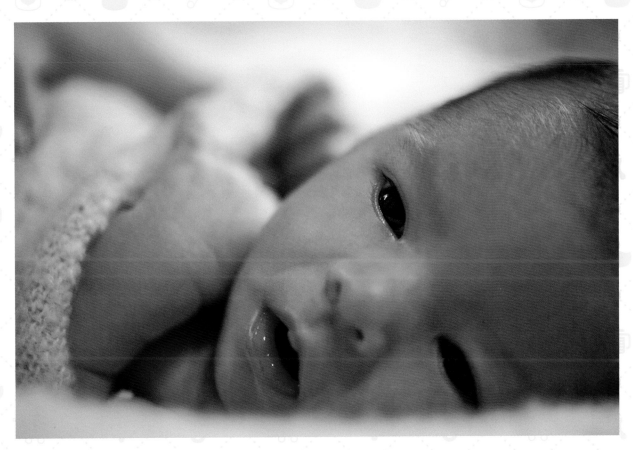

Istock.com/dimarik

Why are my newborn's eyes crossing?

This is one of my favorite questions to answer. This question always shows up around the time a baby is one month old. It is a concern of so many parents that I just automatically answer the question before it even gets asked. I make it into a lighthearted comment and assure them it is normal. A palpable sigh of relief fills the room.

My comment goes something like this: "Have you noticed that your baby's eyes are crossing?" They will almost always say "Yes." I then reply, "It is completely normal and nothing to worry about. It is always worse around the time they are a month old. Sometimes you will swear that their eyes aren't even connected to each other." I then go into the explanation of why it happens, what to expect, and when to worry...

When a baby is born, they can only see about twelve inches away with any clarity. We often say they can see their mom's face while they are breastfeeding. Everything beyond that is movements and shadows. Their vision improves on a daily basis and by the time

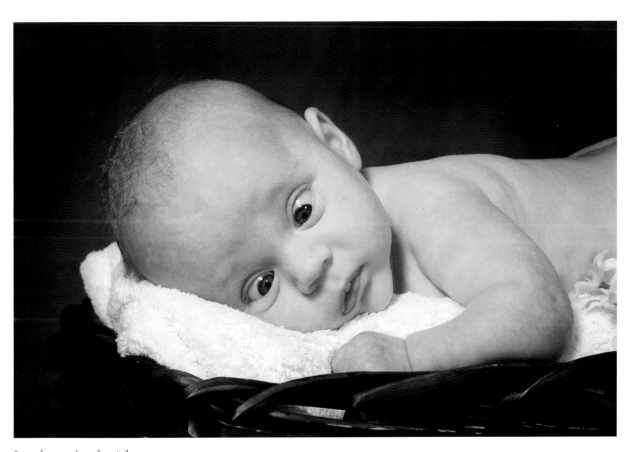

Istock.com/msderrick

they are a month old, they can usually see across the room.

Their eyes are crossing due to a process called accommodation. This is where we go from seeing something far away to something close, or something close to us and then looking into the distance. Babies' eyes haven't figured that out yet. While their eyes are learning it, they will sometimes cross. It looks hilarious when you know what is happening, but it can be terrifying if you are worried about something being wrong with your baby.

The crossing of the eyes is always worse right around the time they are one month old. It is mostly gone by the time they are two months old and we shouldn't see it after they are three months old. There are of course exceptions to this. If you are moving an object your baby is looking at close to their face and between their eyes, their eyes will cross and that is completely normal for all ages if they are staring intently. Another exception is if your baby never seems to focus on anything and their eyes are always crossing or going in different directions. In that instance, we would be worried about your child being blind.

If your baby doesn't seem to focus on anything and their eyes are always crossing, definitely talk to your pediatrician. If their eyes are crossing after they are three months old, that's another talk with your doctor. The most common scenario is for one eye to turn in or out. This may trigger a referral to an eye specialist for further evaluation. For the most part, though, know that it is very common and completely normal in most babies up to one to two months of age.

TAKE-HOME POINTS:

1. Your baby's eyes crossing around the time they are one month old is completely normal and will happen a lot.

2. You should not see their eyes cross after they are three months old, unless something is happening that explains why they crossed their eyes. After three months old, talk to your doctor.

3. If your baby is crossing his eyes often and never seems to focus or see anything, then notify your doctor right away.

Why do my newborn's eyes keep matting shut?

You wake up in the morning and go to take care of a very fussy baby and you notice that her eyes are completely matted shut. She is extremely mad or scared about the fact that she can't seem to open her eyes. You manage to wash out the goo with a washcloth and although her eyes look a little wet, they seem fine. You put her down for a nap and *Boom!* more goo.

This process seems to repeat itself every time your baby goes to sleep. What is going on?

This is most likely nasolacrimal stenosis, a ten-dollar medical word that means a blocked tear duct. It looks gross and the diagnosis sounds serious, but it is very common and very benign.

First off, a baby will not usually have tears that come out of the eye until around the time she is two months old. (Unfortunately, her inability to produce tears has zero impact on her ability to cry.) If you have a newborn that is crying tears, then you most likely have a

Istock.com/Georgiy Datsenko

blocked tear duct. What happens is the normal tears that are produced are drained out of the eye, down the tear duct, into the nasal passageways, and then down the throat. This normal pathway explains why you have a runny nose when you are crying. In the baby with a blocked tear duct, the tears can't drain the way they are supposed to. So, they either come out the eye and look like tears, or they accumulate around the eye when they are asleep. They eventually start to evaporate and form a mucus that mats the eyes shut.

This is extremely common. I see it at least once a day. It will almost always go away on its own, but it is going to take some time. It usually clears up by the time she is nine months old. If she isn't better by nine months, then we will refer the patient to an eye specialist, and she might have a procedure to open up the tear duct. This is very rare, and roughly 99 percent of the time it isn't necessary.

In the meantime, you can take a soft, wet washcloth and massage the inside corner of the eye a couple of times a day for a minute or two. Make sure you put pressure against the nose and not against the eyeball. Will this help? Maybe. The jury is still out on whether this speeds up the resolution or just gives you something to do so you feel like you are helping. We do know that it doesn't hurt anything, and I believe time spent loving and caring for your baby is time well spent.

Is there anything you need to worry about if your baby has a gooey eye? The answer would be, of course, yes. We worry if your baby has been sick and you see the goo in the eye that it could be conjunctivitis, or pink-eye. If your baby's eye is red or swollen, if the outside of the eye looks red or feels hot, or if your baby has a fever, she needs to be seen. Remember, always, *always* treat fevers in newborns as an emergency. See a doctor right away if fever is present.

TAKE-HOME POINTS:

1. A baby that has a tearing eye that mats shut is usually a blocked tear duct and it will usually go away on its own.
2. If your baby has a fever, is acting sick, and has the matted eye, then see your doctor.
3. If your baby's eye looks swollen, feels hot to the touch, and is very fussy, get seen by a doctor pretty fast and consider even an emergency room visit.

Why is it important for my baby to sleep on her back?

Okay, for this one I am taking a break from the jovial tone of this book. This is a serious subject.

The American Academy of Pediatrics has recommended that a baby sleep on its back since 1992. This was the result of the "Back to Sleep" campaign and following this recommendation the incidence of Sudden Infant Death Syndrome (SIDS) fell by 50 percent.

That alone should be enough to close the chapter on this. Yet there is still an unresolved question: Why is that?

To be completely honest, we don't know for sure. There are varying theories on the subject. One theory says that maybe babies that sleep on their belly don't get as much oxygen. The idea is they are rebreathing air in a confined space with a diminishing

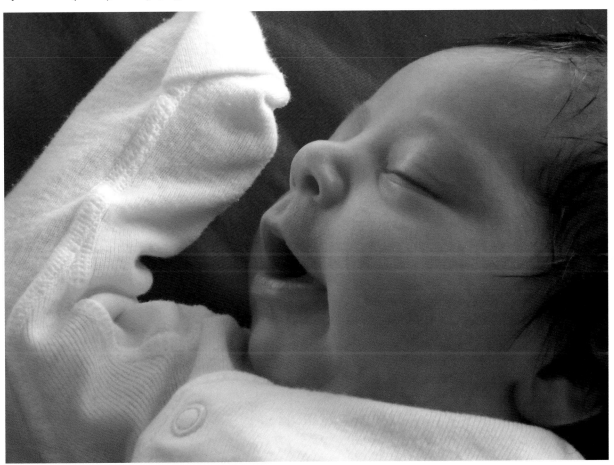

Istock.com/tiburonstudios

oxygen content. Another school of thought is that some babies' brains do not function well in one position or the other. The bottom line is we don't know for sure. We do know we've had half as many deaths due to SIDS since pediatricians began recommending babies be put to sleep on their backs.

What exactly is SIDS? SIDS is defined as an unexpected and unexplained death of a baby less than one year old, usually in his sleep. It is also known as "crib death" just because the baby was usually in a crib when it happened. Although we can't explain the death, research has found that there are certain risk factors that are commonly shared between these babies. It is more likely to happen in boys. The most common age for SIDS is between two and four months of age. Premature babies have a higher risk. It happens more in non-white babies. It is also more common if there are smokers in the house, especially the mother.

There are certain medical conditions that can lead to an increased risk for SIDS as well. Risk factors can include the obvious like prematurity or neurological defects, but even a common cold increases the risk of a baby being affected. If your baby has a severe medical problem and dies during his sleep, this is not commonly called SIDS as he most likely died as a complication of the underlying condition. This could include heart problems, severe lung disease, or severe infections.

The main thing we have found to decrease SIDS is having the baby sleep on his back. There are other environmental things that have been found to help as well. It is recommended that the baby be on a firm mattress.

It is also recommended to keep things like blankets, pillows, and stuffed animals out of his bed or crib. Researchers have found that high room temperatures can increase the risk of SIDS, so don't overheat the baby's room. If your baby is cold, it is recommended that you use warmer sleepers or even sleep sacks.

Unfortunately, there are businesses that prey on parents' fear of SIDS. At this time, there are no devices recommended by pediatricians that have been proven to decrease the incidence of SIDS. Please don't waste money on these items thinking it will prevent SIDS.

Having your baby die in their sleep is a huge fear of all parents. It's one of those things that is unimaginably horrible. Instead of spending lots of money on things that most likely will have no effect on protecting your baby, concentrate on them being in a safe environment with safe sleeping conditions. It's the best thing you can do to protect them.

Just a side note: Have you ever heard the old wives' tale of a cat stealing a baby's breath?

The tale goes as follows: You should never have a cat in the house with a baby because the cat will steal the baby's breath and it will die. The origin of the advice comes from a time when cats were fairly closely associated with witchcraft and thought to be a little evil. A baby that dies from SIDS will typically spit up a little while dying. Since the baby was milk fed and cats often were as well, the smell of the milk would attract the cat. The cat was often found licking the baby's face just as the parents discovered the fact that their baby was no longer breathing. The cats ended up taking the blame for something they didn't have anything to do with.

TAKE-HOME POINTS:

1. Always put your baby to sleep on his back. It is the safest way for him to sleep.
2. Make sure your baby is sleeping on a firm mattress and there aren't any loose sheets, blankets, pillows, or stuffed animals in the bed.
3. Try to avoid having any smoke in the house with the baby.
4. Don't overheat your baby's room.
5. If you have a higher-risk baby due to prematurity or a medical condition, talk to your pediatrician about ways to decrease the risk of SIDS.

Why does my breastfed baby need vitamin D?

Babies were made to drink breast milk. I don't care who you are or what you want to feed your baby, it is futile to dispute the fact that as mammals we were made to drink milk from our mothers. It would make sense that breast milk. would have everything that your baby could ever need. Then you go to your pediatrician and they find out you are going to breastfeed. They tell you to give your baby vitamin D drops every day for as long as you are breastfeeding. If it's perfect for my baby, why do I need to give her anything extra?

This is a very valid question. Basic logic seems to dictate that the vitamin D drops are unnecessary, right? Well, this valid question has an equally valid answer.

The answer is found in history. Waaaaaay back in history, when we lived the way Mother Nature intended us to. Long before central

Istock.com/eli_asenova

90

air conditioning, high-rise office buildings, smartphones, and Wi-Fi.

We lived outside. I know, it is a weird concept today, but just go with it for a minute. Trust me, there was a time in human history when meat and vegetables did not arrive by delivery. You had to go get food. So that is what we did. We were hunters and gatherers. We did most of our daily activities outside and in the sun. As human society became more advanced, we started developing agriculture. This new advancement improved living conditions and laid the groundwork for cities and human culture. Still, even with the rise of agriculture and human civilization, we spent most of our time outside in the sun all day.

You may have noticed I keep mentioning the sun. You see where this is going, don't you?

The sun shined down upon our largely unclothed bodies and our skin converted that sunlight to vitamin D. At that time, mom had a huge amount of vitamin D that she transmitted through the placenta to her unborn baby. This store of vitamin D would last for as long as the baby needed to be wrapped up and kept safe from the elements, but it wasn't long before that baby was running around naked in the sunshine and soaking up her own vitamin D.

Then history started to change and so did our living arrangements and clothing. We started to clothe ourselves and our children. It was no longer "decent" to run around without clothing, so we covered our skin. As we evolved, so did our use of materials. Our buildings changed like those three little pigs'

houses. First straw, then sticks, then finally rocks/stone/bricks. As material science progressed, we may have been able to keep the wolf out, but there was another problem developing while the wolf was held at bay. We had cleverly shielded ourselves from the sun, which we would soon learn had consequences of its own. As humans were spending more and more time indoors, conditions like rickets started to show up. We didn't understand why, so science went to work on finding out. It was because of rickets that a team of researchers discovered how vitamin D is synthesized in our skin.

We discovered that vitamin D is vital to preventing problems like rickets. We found out some other things, too. As science started to study disease states, and medicine started to try and prolong life by disease prevention, we discovered that sun exposure could increase the chances of developing skin cancer. It wasn't long before we started to invent better sunscreen to protect our skin from the harmful rays of the sun.

Ugh. So, no sun, get rickets. Too much sun, get cancer. (Hey, evolution is messy. It takes time to work these things out.)

With each of our societal improvements, we had less and less sun exposure. Less sun exposure leads to fewer chances to make vitamin D on our own. The problem isn't that breast milk didn't have enough vitamin D in it. The issue is it isn't supposed to. We are supposed to get our vitamin D from the sun, and now we are avoiding the sun. Nature had a plan, and we changed it.

Now moms are typically vitamin D deficient, so they don't give the baby that extra store of it prenatally. Babies don't get enough vitamin D through breast milk, or the sun. We started fortifying whole milk and baby formula with vitamin D, but we can't change breast milk.

So, the options are simple. You can return to an agrarian non-modernized society, eschewing all modern conveniences. You can sell all your belongings and live in a hut (preferably near the equator) and adopt a hunter/gatherer lifestyle. I guess if you really must you can still have Wi-Fi, but I don't know when you would be using it, as hunting and gathering requires constant attention. The other option is adding a vitamin D supplement. I'll let you guess which one most people would prefer.

So, what do we actually need vitamin D for?

Vitamin D is essential for strong bones and teeth. It helps in the regulation of our blood sugar and helps us maintain good health. A healthy level of vitamin D helps to prevent cancer. Low levels of vitamin D can lead to increased problems with allergies, eczema, and asthma. We now know that it is also an important regulator of mood. Low levels of vitamin D can make you feel tired, run-down, and even depressed. It is now thought that a substantial part of the population is vitamin D deficient. There is still a lot of research being done tying vitamin D deficiencies to all sorts of conditions.

So, the basics are that we all need vitamin D. Our body is incapable of making it on its own. It is produced when the skin is exposed to sunshine or it can be taken in orally through foods or supplements. With humans taking greater and greater precautions regarding exposing our skin to the sun, it is becoming more important to get our required vitamin D orally. Since we can't add it to breast milk, breastfed babies are recommended to take an extra daily supplement.

TAKE-HOME POINTS:

1. We all need vitamin D.
2. Vitamin D is important for bones, teeth, and good health, as well as mental health and well-being.
3. Breast milk is not deficient in vitamin D. Breast milk was never supposed to deliver the correct amount of vitamin D to babies. It was never the plan. We live in a world deficient in sun exposure.

Why does my baby spit up?

This is a *big* question that has lots of answers, and the answers all depend on how you ask the question. The problem is that spitting up is something that all babies do. It can range from a simple burp where a little milk comes out to a symptom of a serious illness or need for surgery. Spit up ranges from normal, to troubling, to very serious. So, how do you sort out what to do about something every baby will do, and could be of no consequence, or could be life-threatening?

As you read this section, you will need to pay careful attention. This is a doozy of a question, and we are going to tackle it the same way you eat an elephant. You just take it one bite at a time.

Babies are set up to spit up. This is because they drink an entire liquid diet and it is easier to spit up a liquid than it is a thicker solid. They also spend a lot of time lying down. Gravity acts on stomach contents just like it does on us. It pulls everything down toward the ground. Now think about this like a math problem. If a ten-pound baby drinks six ounces, this would be the equivalent to

Istock.com/Anchiy

a 150-pound adult drinking almost three-fourths of a gallon of milk. Take that adult and lay them down and do a bunch of sit-ups and what do you think is going to happen? If they don't hurl, they will at least think about it.

If our stomach is lower than our mouth, then gravity helps pull our food into our stomach. If our mouth is below the level of our stomach, gravity will try and pull it that direction. This is why eating while doing a headstand is not a popular activity. (Well, that and no one has made a viral challenge out of trying it yet. If you're reading this and thinking hey I could . . . *Please just don't, okay?*)

Take a look at your baby while they are lying down. See the gravity problem? Now look at baby's car seat. That buckle puts pressure on their little tummy. That tummy gets squeezed and up comes the milk. Usually on something nice like a designer jacket, or a leather car seat.

In our normal baby with just a normal amount of spit up, we see more spitting up in the first couple of months of life. They are just getting the hang of eating and swallowing and sometimes everything doesn't quite work the way it is supposed to. Think of it as a break-in period. At about a month of age, we will see an increase in spit-up as they eat more frequently due to a growth spurt. Also, they lose the reflex that makes them poop automatically and so they are pushing harder with their abdominal muscles to try and poop. Again, these are new processes in their little bodies, and some break-in time is needed.

So, think about it. The front and back doors of the system are breaking in at varying rates.

Modern necessities like car seats add pressure. Add to that the system architecture being slightly off when they lay down, and a voracious appetite. It's nature's perfect spit-up machine. It's a spit-a-pa-looza. It's spitacular. (If it was possible to take that too far, I think I just did it.)

Between four and six months of age, we may see a little increase in spitting up as well. Yep, you heard me, an *increase*. As they are trying to learn to roll over, they are putting more pressure on their abdomen flexing those muscles. Those core muscles are what they use to roll over, and just like that pesky seat buckle, guess where that puts the pressure. The good news is, once your baby goes through these stages, normal spit-up starts to go away. After that, it will be a very unusual occurrence.

The most common problem that causes spitting up is called reflux. To be honest, any spit-up is technically reflux, but we as pediatricians will reserve the diagnosis of reflux for when it starts to cause problems that require intervention. We narrow down these issues to three problems we see that give us cause for concern.

The first is that the reflux has caused a problem that necessitated a visit to the office or emergency department. These include turning blue, stopping breathing, or an aspiration that led to pneumonia.

The second reason is that the spitting up is of such a large volume that our baby is not growing due to a lack of calories. Your pediatrician will be watching baby's growth and weight and will know if it is not progressing as it should.

The third and the most common is the reflux has led to the baby having pain. Pain in a baby will be manifest as excessive crying, arching their back, or refusing to drink because it hurts.

All three of these require that your doctor try to intervene and help your baby. These interventions could include various ways to feed your baby, perhaps in different positions. They may also suggest different types of milk or food and sometimes even medications.

The second most common problem causing spitting up is a problem with their milk. In the case of breast milk, this may be due to something mom is eating that upsets the baby's stomach or even an allergy to a component of mom's milk. Remember, as mom eats, her body breaks those things down, and they help to create mom's milk. Mom may eat something she is not allergic to, but the baby is.

In formula-fed babies, it can be a problem with the sugar in the milk (lactose) or it can be due to an allergy to one of the proteins in the milk. These can be addressed with a change in type of formula. This is something about which you should always seek out advice from your pediatrician, as all formulas are not created equal and different types address different kinds of problems.

The third type of problem that could lead to spitting up is an illness or serious condition. These will usually present as a sudden change and will usually be a much more violent vomiting rather than just a little spit-up. A good rule of thumb is, if a baby less than two months of age is having large amounts of vomit, he needs to see the doctor or the emergency department right away.

If the spitting up is getting worse with each feed and getting to be larger in volume, or further in reach, you need to see a doctor quickly.

Most of the time you will see more than just spitting up in these situations. If your baby has a fever, acts lethargic, is crying in pain, has any odd movements, or is just not acting right, then see a doctor as soon as possible. The illnesses and conditions that can cause spitting up in a baby can be very serious and can cause big problems very quickly. These are situations that may require surgery to correct. Do not let these go on! Make sure a doctor sees a baby presenting any of these issues.

This is a big topic, and a good place to start with all diagnosis is with the attitude of the baby. A good rule of thumb is to look at happy vs. upset. A little spit-up in a happy baby is not a big deal and is almost always normal. A lot of spit-up, with a sick-acting baby or a very upset baby should cause you to look closer and see your doctor as soon as possible.

TAKE-HOME POINTS:

1. Spitting up in your baby is very common . . . they will spit up!
2. Spitting up in a baby is predictable and will get a little worse before it gets better but will pretty much disappear by the time they are six months old or so.
3. If you have a baby who is in pain, turns blue, quits breathing, has a fever, acts sick, or isn't growing, then you need to have a doctor looking at your baby and figuring out what is going on.
4. Remember, a little spit, happy baby, probably okay. A lot of spit, unhappy baby, or sick baby, see a doctor.

Why is my baby going bald?

This is usually one of those fun questions to answer. Parents are worried about the fact that their baby is losing hair. Hey, bald is beautiful, right? Just think of Vin Diesel, Bruce Willis, Squidward, The Rock, the list goes on. There is a very benign reason for it happening and it is completely normal . . . most of the time.

We are going to divide this answer into three categories based on age. Specific things happen at specific growth stages, and knowing that helps you understand what is happening and . . . *why*.

Let's talk about newborns first. Say your baby is born with a bald spot. This is the only one that is usually going to get my attention. If your baby has a lot of hair and they have a very distinct bald spot that has well-defined borders and no sign of hair in the middle, this is most likely alopecia areata. This is hair loss that can happen at birth or later and is an autoimmune problem (meaning your body is attacking itself). This will usually get a referral to a dermatologist, because properly treated most will have some hair regrowth and 50 percent will have complete hair regrowth. This can be corrected with a surgery later on if needed to remove the portion of the scalp without hair.

Istock.com/jfairone

The next type of hair loss in a baby can occur in the first several months of life. This is commonly seen in babies born with lots of dark hair. Sometimes the parents are wondering where the dark hair came from. Well, *surprise!* They are really going to have light-colored hair, it just isn't here yet. The hair starts to fall out on the top, leaving a ring around the sides and back. Then hair will start to regrow, but it is a lighter color. This is not a cause for alarm at all and happens all the time. The only pain and suffering that happens is sometimes the parents really thought the dark hair was adorable.

Another common cause of hair loss in a baby happens between the time they are two and six months of age. This will happen in the back of their scalp and present as an oval shaped area of hair loss.

If you think hard, you might be able to guess this one. I'll give you a hint—roll.

Give up?

This happens as a baby is learning to roll over and they rub their head from side to side. The friction of their head rubbing on whatever they are lying on will rub out the hair. This hair will grow back as soon as the baby learns to roll over and quits doing the side-to-side motion of their head.

Some babies will suffer hair loss from them pulling on their hair constantly. Just like there are babies that suck on their thumb or constantly want to be touching a blanket, there are babies that will pull or twist their hair. In turn, the constant traction and friction of the scalp will cause the hair to fall out. This will stop as they grow up and terminate the behavior.

Rarely, hair loss in a baby is due to illness or infection. Very rarely babies can develop psoriasis in the scalp, which can lead to bald spots with dry, flaky skin underneath. The area will be red and irritated as well. They can also lose hair due to an infection. Fungal infections like ringworm can cause hair breakage and thinning. A skin infection from bacteria can cause hair loss and the underlying skin will look red and oozing. Any of these conditions should be examined and treated by a physician.

Although there are several reasons for a baby to lose hair, the benign ones are the most common. A good rule of thumb is if the skin of the scalp doesn't look normal, then you should get a doctor to look at it right away. If the skin looks normal underneath, it will either be completely benign or something that is more chronic and doesn't need immediate attention.

TAKE-HOME POINTS:

1. A lot of babies lose hair, and it is most likely a completely benign process and their hair will come back.
2. If they look like your uncle on your mom's side with hair just in the back and on the sides, it is normal.
3. Consult with your doctor if your baby has bald spots they are born with or if there is a rash on the skin where the hair is missing.

Why does my baby have dandruff?

Welcome to the world of cradle cap, or as I like to call it, "cradle crap." I have a lot of concerned parents wondering about this stuff and how to make it go away.

My advice is simple. Other than looking ugly, it really doesn't cause too many problems. It eventually goes away. Be like The Beatles, and "Let It Be."

Cradle cap, just like any medical condition, has a medical name that is hard to pronounce: seborrheic dermatitis. (Honestly, that sounds awful doesn't it? Hello Joan, how is the little bundle of joy? What? Seborrheic Dermatitis? *Oh no!! How can it be?*)

In regular everyday terms, this is what we call dandruff. Cradle cap/dandruff in a baby

Istock.com/russaquarius

is fairly predictable in its course and how it presents. Pediatricians tend to refer to it as cradle cap for the first four months of life and then call it dandruff or seborrheic dermatitis afterward.

Cradle cap usually starts around the time a baby is three to five weeks old. It starts off being a red bumpy rash, appearing on the upper chest or face. The red rash will spread upward and start forming red bumps up on the scalp. After the bumps form, a scaly dry rash begins that may be white, yellow, or orange in color. The severity of the rash and flakes vary from one baby to another, but usually the babies who have a worse rash will have worse flakes. The flakes can range from just a fine little dry skin scale to very thick yellow scales. For most babies, this whole process will last two to eight weeks, but some babies will have it up to a year and a few babies have it forever, as it just becomes classic dandruff.

Good news! Other than looking ugly, it very rarely causes any problems. Probably the most common problem seen is the rash on the face and scalp makes the skin much easier to scratch and bleed. Because the skin is irritated from the rash, it makes it very itchy for the baby. Combine that with razor blade-sharp fingernails and you can end up with some pretty vicious-looking scratches. The other problem we sometimes encounter is the scale can get so thick behind the ears that it can lead to sores that can crack and bleed.

To be honest, there aren't any great treatments for cradle cap. The treatment is usually benign neglect. Just leave it alone and it will eventually go away. Yet for most parents, an ugly rash on your otherwise cute little baby can't go untreated. Because of this, parents throughout the ages have sought ways to "cure" cradle cap.

Treatment #1 is the most benign. Use a gentle shampoo and gently scrub the area with the flakes. Be very gentle in the scrubbing. Remember your baby has a soft spot and they have very sensitive skin. Don't make the "cure" worse than the "disease." Try not to over-bathe or wash too much or you will cause your baby to have drier skin that can lead to more dandruff.

Treatment #2 is the one I hear the most from parents or see on the Internet. Use some baby lotion or petroleum jelly on the scalp and scrub with a toothbrush or a soft brush. This actually works pretty well in getting rid of the flakes, but just realize that they are going to come back. There is not an actual cure for cradle cap; there are only ways to make it look a little better or control it.

Treatment #3 involves your doctor. Your baby has developed a severe rash that is cracking, bleeding, or causing sores. Your doctor is usually going to prescribe a dandruff shampoo or a steroid cream to help heal the sores and help the rash out a bit.

Treatment #4 usually comes when the baby hasn't had her cradle cap resolved by four months of age. This is when most doctors start recommending the use of some over-the-counter dandruff shampoos. Make sure you listen to your doctor on how often to use it (I usually recommend twice a week) and any safety information (like preventing it from getting in your baby's eyes).

Overall, dandruff or cradle c(r)ap is very common and usually very benign. The cases that require your doctor's help are rare. There are things that you can do to make it look better and to take care of the problems it creates. You can do things to ease the irritation if it is making baby itchy. The bad news is it will last as long as it wants to last, as there isn't a cure.

1. That red bumpy rash on your baby's face is much more likely to be the start of cradle cap than baby acne.
2. Cradle cap usually starts between three and five weeks of age and usually lasts two to eight weeks.
3. If your baby develops sores or is miserable with cradle cap, consult your pediatrician.
4. There are things to make it look better, but be safe and careful with your baby. Too much "treatment" can make things worse.

Why is my child sucking his thumb?

"Seriously, the thumb-sucking is driving me crazy!" one parent told me. "There has got to be a way to stop this. Why is this even a thing?" Again, in the list of questions that should have made me a millionaire by now, this is near the top. After convincing this parent there was no malicious plot between the child's peer group to slowly drive them to insanity with the gentle to ferocious sound of thumb-sucking, my answer was a less than satisfactory "They want to." I think that may have lumped me in with the conspirators in the parent's eyes.

My answer, which is totally correct, is usually not what parents are looking for. Let's begin with the right questions.

1. How can I get my kid to stop?
2. Should I be worried?
3. Is this going to cause some long-term harm?

If your first search for answers is online, you're likely to come across something that sounds like it came from some crystal healer whose website touts the benefits of soaking baby's feet in tea, poop, or some other woo woo. Use positive reinforcement, gentle reminders, and a calming responsive parental patience. Ahhhhh. How nice. Now you'll pardon me while I vomit.

Understand that many babies are sucking their thumbs while still in the womb. It's a self-soothing behavior usually accompanied by stress, sadness, or a lack of sleep. It's normal, and it is perfectly healthy. You may substitute the thumb-sucking for a pacifier, but that will just be something different you will need to take away from him.

That said, eventually there will be a time when this activity needs to stop. Pediatric dentists say that thumb-sucking after the age of two could affect the shape of the upper palate (roof of the mouth), the angle of the jaw affecting their baby teeth and, potentially, permanent teeth. This is a perfectly good reason to stop thumb-sucking.

But how do we stop this? The short answer is don't worry about it. The idea of positive reinforcement and gentle reminders is great, but I think it's unnecessary. I think it's all right to describe the thumb as a nasty place via which germs and dirt look for ways to enter the body to promote illness. Dipping the thumb into vinegar or hot sauce (not too hot) so it tastes nasty is good too. There are some online products like thumb guards or thumb gloves that also work pretty well. I ended up putting multiple Band-Aids on my son's thumb, and he stopped in three days.

Some medical folks have said these tactics can permanently scar your child. This is classically referred to as "psychobabble." Personally, I say let them suck their thumb in peace until about 18 months. At around a year and a half of age, work on getting them to stop. Your child will be fine. If you can get

Istock.com/energyy

them to stop soon enough to avoid braces, you can start saving for your Ferrari.

Other long-term effects of thumb-sucking include: damage to the thumbnail, which can in fact be permanent; infections along the edge of the nail; dry peeling skin that can be extremely uncomfortable to even painful due to the skin breakdown from constantly being wet and the trauma from teeth; and even bullying from other children due to thumb-sucking. None of these are great problems to have, but they are extremely uncommon. Most of these little critters are going to suck their thumbs when they are tired, stressed, or bored and the rest of the time those little thumbs are being used to get into all kinds of problems that only people with opposable thumbs can do.

TAKE-HOME POINTS:

1. Thumb-sucking is completely normal and often starts before your baby is even born.
2. I have no problem trying to give a baby a pacifier instead of his thumb. It is easier to take away a pacifier than it is a thumb.
3. Don't freak out. We want to try and get it to stop by the time the baby is 18 months. If he is over 18 months old and still sucking his thumb, don't freak out. He will eventually stop. If he doesn't stop, he will hide it. In the big world of bad stuff, if thumb-sucking is the worst of the baby's problems, you win.

Why did my baby get thrush?

Okay, if you are a brand-new parent that may not be the first question you have. The first question might be, what is thrush? It's a good question, and probably one that even seasoned parents don't know the complete answer to.

Thrush is a fungal infection found in the mouth. It is caused by the fungus Candida albicans and can also be called "Candidiasis" (usually by doctors who like big words and want to sound smart). When we use the term "infection," it sounds so ominous and contagious. The truth is that Candida albicans normally resides in our mouth and our skin and usually doesn't cause any trouble. It is really an overgrowth of the fungus that causes us any pain or suffering.

A thrush infection, or the overgrowth of the Candida albicans, happens when there is something that sets off the normal balance.

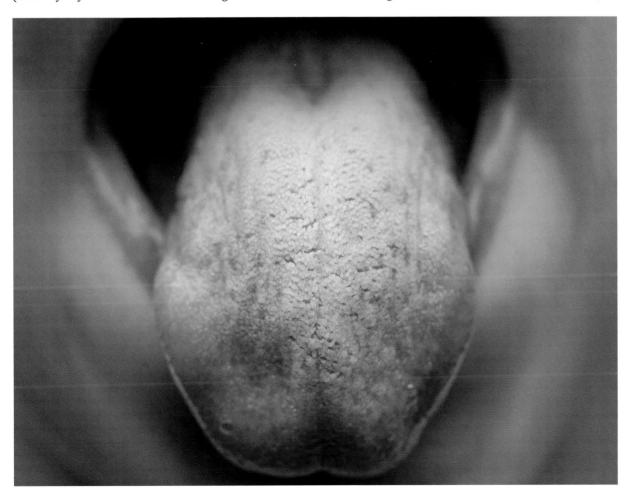

Istock.com/canbedone

The most common age at which one could get a thrush infection is a young baby or the elderly. This is because in these two age groups their immune system is naturally weakened, and they are unable to keep the growth of the fungus to its normal levels. We can also see overgrowth of Candida if we have been on antibiotics, have diabetes, have cancer, or are being treated for cancer. Autoimmune disorders like HIV also can be the cause of a breakout.

For the scope of our book, there are usually going to be one of three scenarios causing thrush. The first is just typical for newborns, usually in the first couple months of life. It just happens. There wasn't really anything that you did wrong as a parent. There's nothing really wrong with the baby. The normal balance of bacteria and yeast in the mouth gets out of whack. The Candida albicans starts growing and takes over.

The second scenario is when a baby has been on antibiotics for an infection. The antibiotic kills good bacteria as well as bad, and it allows the Candida to overgrow and cause thrush.

The third scenario is hopefully something you never encounter. Thrush can flourish in a child with a weakened immune system, for a child suffering from HIV or cancer, or anything that compromises their immunity.

What you see with thrush is a white plaque that is usually found on the gums, the sides of the mouth, the back of the throat, the roof of the mouth, and the top of the tongue. Babies will usually be fussy and not feed as well because it causes some pain. If you were to scrape the white plaque off the surface of the mouth, it would be bright red underneath and you could even see some mild bleeding. This would be different from just milk stuck to the surface of the mouth or tongue that could easily be scraped off and would just leave normal skin underneath.

Candida albicans can cause some other problems besides just thrush in the mommy-baby duo. Because it is in the baby's mouth, the baby can pass it to mom's breast. During breastfeeding, Candida has the perfect environment to cause an infection in mom. Candida likes wet environments and it tries to get into cracks in the skin to cause infections. This can lead to red, cracking, and very painful nipples and areola and even more widespread on the breast. Babies can also swallow the Candida and it will go through the GI tract and come out in the stool. It can then lead to a terrible diaper rash on the other end. Again, a perfect environment made up of moisture and cracking, dry skin for it to set up shop and lead to a very painful diaper rash.

When a baby has a thrush infection or a yeast diaper rash, or if mom develops yeast on the breast, it is time to enlist some help from your pediatrician. The pediatrician will confirm the diagnosis usually just from looking at the mouth or rash. There are occasions that scrapings can be made to confirm the diagnosis under a microscope, but that is very rare. Treatment usually consists of an antifungal medication. This medication comes in an oral form that can be applied to the spots on the inside of the mouth and as an ointment that can be applied to the skin in the case of a rash. Usually you want to treat until the rash or thrush is gone and then continue to treat for two more days to make sure it doesn't come back.

If your baby continues to get thrush over and over again, your pediatrician should consider a work-up to rule out any immune problems that could affect the baby's ability to fight off infection. This is something that is very rare, but most pediatricians will have a couple in their career that have some sort of problem that needs to be addressed.

Why am I so tired if my baby sleeps sixteen to twenty hours a day?

I remember the day well. Our youngest, Kaden, was almost a month old. I looked over at my wife, Kristi, and saw two of her. I told both of them that I was pretty sure we were going to die.

This is an oh-so-familiar story, isn't it? It's the thing bad sitcoms use to paint a caricature of a tired, stressed parent. They give them heavy eyelids, a dopey/punch-drunk disposition, and a disheveled appearance. The laugh track rolls. Yeah, well, it's not so funny when your baby has colic and has been screaming for what seems like an eternity. Day becomes night. Hours fade, sometimes days. You end up actively wondering if this is what madness feels like. Did I shower today? What day is it? Who am I?

I see this scenario play out in front of me almost every day. Parents come in the office with very little babies and look like they have been tortured. I'm not sure whether to look at the actual patient, or notify Amnesty International.

Istock.com/alexxx1981

Let's be honest, what a newborn puts their parents through is probably a violation of the Geneva Convention and an illegal form of torture. They constantly cry, then they let you go to sleep only to wake you up minutes later. This nefarious cycle plays on repeat for days, weeks, or even months. This induces a level of stress most humans aren't ready for, unless they're trained Special Forces members. As a bonus, they increase your workload, adding tasks you may be unfamiliar with. These new tasks all involve a tiny human that has propensity for hysterical outbursts. The tiny human has a limited ability to communicate, but he tends to be critical of your performance, nonetheless. The tiny human can (and likely will) poop and pee on you, vomit on you, and expel a few other fluids here and there. Mind you, the unwanted dousing in these foul items is not a method of criticism. Oh, no. These are simply things that just happen in the normal, daily course of events.

All of this comes while you still need to do all the things that you had to do before. Oh yeah, remember that life you had before the baby? It's still there. No one started doing it all for you. It's not like you had a baby, then dropped back by the office and everyone is like "Hey, you're a mom now. It's cool, we'll keep paying you, but we'll take care of your job from now on." You still have work, laundry, cooking, cleaning, and possibly other kids to take care of. It would be nice to have a free couple of minutes to shower, or maybe go to the bathroom. Yes, even bathroom breaks can be considered a luxury when you have a newborn.

We've all read the baby books. We read the part that says a newborn baby should sleep 16 to 20 hours a day. As a pediatrician, I have reassured thousands of parents that it was okay that their baby was sleeping all the time. So, if they are asleep 16 to 20 hours a day, why are we about to die from sleep deprivation? Shouldn't we be able to sleep at the same time and get 16 to 20 hours of sleep as well? Nope!

There are lots of factors involved here, of course. Let's start with the most obvious—the division of labor. The baby only needs to eat, pee, poop, and sleep. That pretty much describes their days for the first couple of months of life. You however need to eat, sleep, pee, poop, plus somehow find the time to make food for you and the baby. Don't forget there's all the laundry, which increased with the baby. You also need to bathe (both yourself and the baby), shop for all the normal stuff, plus purchase the gargantuan list of baby supplies. Chances are that someone in the house (possibly both of you) still needs to work, and the amount of time to sleep goes down a lot.

Second in the list is the visitors. It will seem to happen at the wrong time, every time. Just at the moment that you could sneak in a little catnap, someone drops by to see how you are doing. Oh, they come under the guise of being helpful, maybe they even drop by a little present or even some food. In the process they would really like to see the baby, talk to you, and swap some baby stories. When they finally leave, the window for sleep is gone, the house needs to be straightened again, and there are more dishes to wash.

The third reason is you may have other kids who need time and attention as well. They may have homework, ball games, practices, or need to be taken to school. They for sure generate laundry. They need to be fed, bathed, cleaned up after, and they keep pointing out that you are ignoring them because you are busy taking care of the baby. Now all the time that you aren't taking care of the baby you need to pay attention to them or you will feel like the worst parent ever.

The fourth reason could be the spouse. Let's just do what normally happens anyway and just ignore them. After all they are adults, right? Wrong! They are sleepy, tired, overworked, and stressed out just like you. The only support they are going to get is from you. The same goes for you . . . they are your only hope. The hope starts to look a little shaky when your best chance for help looks and feels the same as you.

Finally, there is this little fact of differing sleep cycles. You have probably heard of sleep cycles in terms of light sleep, deep sleep, and REM sleep. We do not need to go deeper into sleep cycles than that. Just know that a sleep cycle takes time to go through all the stages of sleep. In order for sleep to be effective, we need to go through all the stages of sleep. Your sleep cycle is very slow and may only go through two to four cycles of sleep stages a night. Baby's sleep cycle is very fast and goes through many more cycles than an adult does. That means that when a baby wakes up at the end of their sleep cycle and wants to eat, get changed, be played with, or just get up for the day, there is a good chance you are not done with your sleep cycle. Studies have shown that if you prevent a person from completing their sleep cycle, they will start to suffer from exhaustion despite getting sleep. Eventually you can start to go a little crazy.

It all starts to make sense, doesn't it? The reason that you feel so tired is there is no time to sleep and when you do go to sleep you don't get to complete a sleep cycle. What do you need to do?

Get help!

Divide and conquer with your partner. Try to make sure that both of you are getting some quality sleep. Call in reinforcements from the grandparents. Do whatever you need to do to survive. Pride will not cut it here. It's okay to ask for help. I wish more parents did.

TAKE-HOME POINTS:
1. You are exhausted because you are not getting enough sleep.
2. You are tired because the sleep you are getting is not good sleep.
3. It is perfectly okay to ask for help.

Why does my baby need to eat so frequently?

As a pediatrician I get asked this fairly often. As a dad I was asking this question about every two to three hours. All of you that have been through this are likely nodding along at this point. If this is your first foray into the sleep-deprived world of feeding a newborn, welcome. It may seem really stressful at first, but not to worry. You'll lose so much sleep you probably won't remember much of it later, anyway.

There are several reasons why newborns in particular need very regular feedings on short intervals. I bet you're wondering how you can change it. Make some adjustments, stretch it out a bit?

You can't. Sorry.

They have good reasons for their appetite, and none of them are things you can do anything about. Those little ones need the regular feeding. It's very important. Why? Glad you asked.

First, they have a tiny stomach and can only take in a little bit at a time. The common comparison is that a newborn has a stomach the size of a golf ball. They are growing and need calories. If you can't eat large meals, then you eat a lot of meals. Babies are using a tremendous amount of energy (relative to their size). They need to grow and keep warm

Istock.com/miodrag ignjatovic

and occasionally squirm around a bit. They don't have energy reserves yet, so food is the only source. Therefore, they need food frequently and they need lots of it.

Speaking of energy reserves, babies don't have very efficient storage systems in general. They don't have a huge stockpile of fat or glycogen. We all understand the concept of fat and mostly how it compels us to shop for new pants when we don't want to. Glycogen, however, is something most of us don't understand. Glycogen is strands of glucose our bodies store in the liver, where it can be accessed quickly. Babies do have some stores of glycogen, but they don't have the same amount as older children or adults.

Finally, sometimes babies just like to eat so they can be close to you. This is especially true for breastfed babies who just like the feeling of being close and snuggly with their mom. Might as well have a snack while I'm here!

The take-home message is they really do need to eat that frequently. You as the parent should not be trying to do anything to change that. Please do not give them anything that someone has recommended will make them sleep longer or eat less frequently. Being a parent is not for the faint of heart or the weak, but we all seem to make it through in the end.

Babies will have a little growth spurt around the time they are three to five weeks old and may even want to eat more frequently. It is important to let them eat. They will usually slow down after a couple of weeks and will eat more per feeding but less frequently. They usually will start to slow down around the time they are two months old, and some will even start to sleep through the night. (I saw that. You gasped and got your hopes up. Sorry again, there's no guarantees here. Their feeding and sleeping habits will change when they need them to. Go with the flow, and enjoy the ride.)

One last time, do not try to make changes. Feed your baby when they ask to be fed.

The only thing I recommend doing that may make a difference eventually is schedule. The more scheduled your life is, the more they will start to fit into your schedule. Try as much as possible to have their bedtime be the same every night and their naps at the same time. Bath time and feedings should also be at a scheduled time. The more things happen at the same time every day, the faster they will get on a schedule that can be predicted.

TAKE-HOME POINTS:

1. In the beginning you will be trying to encourage your baby to eat frequently.
2. After the first five days or so, your baby will want to eat every two to three hours.
3. Around a month of age, they get where they eat every three to four hours with a little growth spurt where they may want to eat every two hours for a week or two.
4. Around the time they are two months of age, they may start going longer between meals . . . mostly at night (at least you can hope).
5. The only thing you can do to help your situation is to try to make their schedule consistent each day.

Why has my baby stopped pooping and started crying like he is in pain?

Ahhh, poop. My old friend. I bet when you were buying this book, you weren't expecting this percentage of poop, were you?

Fair enough. I didn't know pediatrics was going to be so poop-centric either.

This has got to be the most frequently asked question in this entire book. I swear that this will be asked or at least thought about by every parent who has had a baby. That should tell you right there that it is something that is

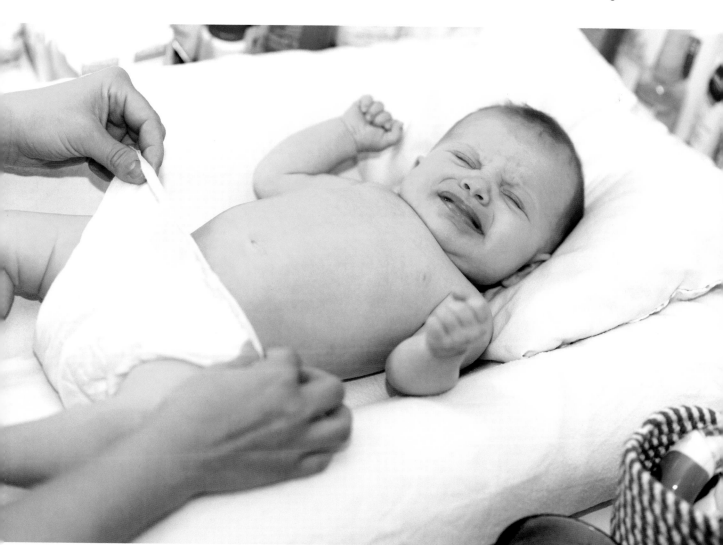

Istock.com/thodonal

very normal and nothing to worry about, but all parents worry about it anyway. Worrying is an inescapable part of becoming a parent. It's not a bad thing, either. Worrying can be very beneficial at times.

This is very likely not one of those times.

I often say that I didn't realize that I was going into pediatrics so that I could become an expert in poop, but poop is what I get to talk about a lot. I embrace it. Honestly, it was tough at first, but now I am happy to share my poop knowledge with the world.

When a baby first starts eating, they have a very active gastrocolic reflex. This reflex causes the colon (large intestine) to contract whenever the stomach gets full. This will mean that your newborn will pretty much poop at least once every time they eat. After the first three to four weeks of changing a diaper after every feed, parents get used to it. It becomes routine—the food goes in, the food comes out. Any change in routine can be cause for alarm, and then comes the worrying.

Somewhere between the ages of three and five weeks, the reflex that makes them poop without effort goes away. Suddenly, we have a baby who does not know how to poop and needs to. I am assuming they know they need to poop. They must feel the need to poop, but it doesn't just happen automatically anymore. So here we have a tiny, growing human that needs to acquire a new skill.

This happens the way it does with most new skills. First, there is denial. They just stop pooping. That is only going to last so long. It usually lasts just long enough for the parents to notice that it has been awhile since they changed a dirty diaper. The questions start

flying around. "Did you change a dirty diaper today? When was the last dirty diaper you changed?" Then they may start to worry and when they worry, I get a phone call.

The next thing the baby is going to do is try very hard to get the poop out. They will start to strain. They have no idea which muscles they need to push to get the poop out, so they try to push them all. They will start to make awful faces, grunt, and turn bright red. Sometimes they get lucky and push the right muscles. Sometimes it takes them forever.

Now if they get lucky and find the right muscles, then they are back to pooping and all is well. It's when they can't quite figure it out that things head south. Babies have one method of communication. So perhaps they're angry, sad, or frustrated. (I can't tell you which emotion they are experiencing. I'm not a psychologist, I'm a poop expert, remember?) Regardless of what emotion they are feeling, they express it with crying.

This is usually when I am going to get a phone call. I fully understand why. I mean, after all, we have discovered that our baby has stopped pooping. Babies do like three things, so if one stops that can be a big deal. Additionally, they are turning bright red and screaming and now they are crying in what must be terrible pain. It is time to get the doctor involved! We must help out the poor little baby.

Now, here we are. The moment of poop truth. Remember when I said I loved this question?

It is now time for me as the doctor to figure out if something really is wrong, or is this a baby who is just mad because she hasn't figured out how to poop? I will have questions for you. The questions are going to go something like this:

1. How long has it been since the baby has pooped?
2. When it came out the last time, was it hard like little round balls?
3. Has there been any blood in the stools?
4. After the baby pooped, did she stop crying and feel better?
5. Has the baby been spitting up more?
6. When she takes her bottle, does it seem like it hurts her to swallow?
7. Is she arching and doing back bends while she is crying?

I know it seems like a lot of questions, but I need to earn my money somehow. We have several things that can happen during this stage of development, and we need to find out which one it is. Do we need to worry? Do we need to do anything different? The typical baby who just needs to learn how to poop is going to strain, turn bright red, pass a lot of gas, and then pass a normal stool and be happy right afterward until the next time she needs to poop. A baby with reflux may be crying a lot and turning red, but with other indicators of a bigger issue. She cries with eating, spits up a lot, arches her back, and pooping doesn't help. A baby with colic cries and turns red, but pooping doesn't make them feel any better. The baby with a milk-protein allergy is just pitiful. Nothing makes her feel any better and she may have blood in her stool. The constipated baby is going to have hard stools that are painful to pass as well as gas pain from the stool sitting in the colon for too long.

You can see there are several things it can be, and it is not your job as a parent to figure it all out. There is a reason I became an expert on poop . . . I needed to so I could help you take care of your baby.

TAKE-HOME POINTS:

1. Around a month of age, a baby will lose the reflex that makes her poop automatically.
2. When this happens, she will push, strain, turn bright red, and pass a lot of gas.
3. It normally takes about two weeks for her to figure out how to poop without making an entire production out of the whole process.
4. Your doctor's job is to rule out problems like constipation, reflux, colic, and milk-protein allergies.
5. Please ask your pediatrician for their thoughts on poop. We're experts, after all.

Why can't I use sunscreen on my newborn?

Wait a second! I thought sunscreen was good. What voodoo is this!?

I thought children had a higher risk of their sun exposure leading to skin cancer. Shouldn't we be protecting babies even more than everyone else from sunburn? How does that even make sense?

Hold those horses a moment. Let's slow down a little and put some things into perspective.

First of all, *yes*. You are absolutely correct in thinking that we should be protecting small babies from the sun even more than everyone else. Their skin is delicate and easily damaged by too much sun. We believe that so strongly that we don't even want them in the sun at all.

If at all possible, your baby should not be out in the sun, especially between the hours of 10 a.m. and 4 p.m. when the sun's ultraviolet rays are at their most dangerous. We want your baby either out of the sun or in the shade and covered up as much as possible if he is going to be out when it's sunny.

So why do we preach the sunscreen for everyone and yet we don't want to put it on newborns?

Istock.com/FamVeld

Most pediatricians, along with the FDA and about every other regulatory or advising agency out there, are not going to recommend sunscreen until your baby is at least four to six months of age. The reason for that is that a baby's skin is very different than older children's or adults' skin. A baby has a higher surface area that can be exposed, and his skin is much more sensitive. Not enough studies have been done on small babies to show that the chemicals in sunscreen are safe when newborns absorb them through their skin.

But wait, there's more!

Babies don't handle heat very well. One of the defense mechanisms that humans have against the heat is sweating. We sweat so the moisture on our skin evaporates and cools us down. Babies can't effectively sweat until they're a little older. Usually around four to six months of age is when they can sweat enough in response to heat to cool themselves down effectively. You also have to remember that your three-month-old can't speak up and say, "Hey, I'm hot. Did you bring anything to drink?" Babies less than six months old are much more likely to get heat stroke or suffer dehydration if exposed to hot temperature for any length of time.

So, if your baby is going to be outside in the warm months of the year, we recommend a few things. First, try to avoid the hottest parts of the day. Keep your baby in the shade—perhaps under an umbrella or a tent. Keep your baby's skin and head covered (hats always look cute in the summer on small babies). Keep your baby well hydrated by offering breast milk or formula frequently. If there is no way to avoid exposure to the sun, make sure you discuss safe options of sunscreen for your baby.

After a baby is four to six months of age and it's safe to use sunscreen, make sure you use a brand that has been tested and approved for babies. Ask your pediatrician if you need help. (We love talking about sunscreen. Really, even more than poop.)

Always remember that most skin cancer is believed to be from skin damage that occurs when we are very young. That means you as a parent have all the power and the responsibility to prevent sun exposure and possibly cancer. This is not a burden you should take lightly.

TAKE-HOME POINTS:

1. Don't use sunscreen until a baby is at least four to six months of age.
2. Ask your doctor about when to use sunscreen and what type to use.
3. Avoid letting your young baby be exposed to direct sunlight, especially between the hours of 10 a.m. and 4 p.m.
4. If your baby is going to be outside, make sure he is in the shade and his skin is covered and protected.
5. If you ever see your baby start to look sunburned, get him out of the sun and try to cool their skin down as soon as possible.
6. When your baby is old enough to use sunscreen, use it liberally and often.

Why isn't my husband bonding with the baby?

First off, men and women are fundamentally different. When a woman thinks of a baby, she thinks warm snuggles, feeding the baby, bathing the baby, and caring for the baby. When a man thinks of a baby, he thinks, *I need to make sure that baby has everything it could possibly need and that I provide for it and my wife better than my dad did*. This different perspective on the needs of the baby will set up some of these bonding issues. Mommy will see that daddy is throwing himself into his work as a way to avoid snuggling the baby. Daddy sees himself throwing himself into his work as a way to show that he truly loves his wife and wants to take care of his baby. (This is the point where we can either stay on topic, or switch gears and go into the whole Mars/Venus thing. Let's stay on task, shall we? Someone else already wrote the Mars/Venus book.)

Next, mommies get a head start in the whole bonding-with-the-baby game. Mommies get to feel the baby move and kick and get the experience of knowing a baby is growing inside of them. Daddies get to see the process happen, but it is very different. Think about the difference of seeing someone in Hawaii via video vs. being in Hawaii

Istock.com/courtneyk

experiencing it for yourself. It is nowhere near the same experience. Usually, moms have already bonded significantly with their baby before the baby ever takes its first breath.

We then have a whole cultural change going on that takes awhile to even out. For the most part, most men who are adults now were primarily cared for by their mother. Traditionally it was the moms who were feeding the children, bathing them, changing them, and doing the daily care of the baby and then kids. Dad spent his days working and coming home late. This is the culture in which your husband or significant other was raised.

There is a good chance he didn't spend much time caring for small children growing up, due to societal norms of the time. Little boys often want to grow up to be just like dad, whereas girls were traditionally going to help with their younger siblings, just like mommy. Young girls regularly took on jobs like babysitting. Now, culturally, we are seeing a change. Men today are taking a more hands-on approach to child-rearing, but are going at it mostly blind. (This is a fantastic development, by the way. Seeing a cultural shift where dad is allowed to express more emotion and truly revel in the joy babies bring is a wonderful thing in my humble opinion.)

So enough of the explanation; when is daddy going to actually bond with the baby?

It varies from family to family, but for the most part I see it happen around the time the baby is two to four months old. At two to four months old, a baby starts to interact more with its environment. They can recognize people, they can smile, they can laugh, and they can reach for someone or grab a finger. I love to watch when it happens. The daddy comes home from work one day and the baby starts bouncing up and down, smiling, and reaching for its daddy. That is the moment that he is hooked. He picks up the baby and knows that he will do anything it takes to protect that baby from harm and make sure it has everything it could ever need.

Babies need lots of stuff. We like to say that babies just need love, but it is difficult to feed them love, dress them in love, and keep them warm and dry under love. Money and support pairs wonderfully with love for a happy baby and family. When you are looking at daddy to see if he is bonding with the baby, don't just tally the score based on snuggles or number of diapers changed. Put the whole picture together and you will probably find that he has bonded with that baby a lot more than you are giving him credit for.

TAKE-HOME POINTS:

1. When it comes to bonding with your baby, just remember that mommy got a head start.
2. Daddies often bond by taking care of the financial needs of the family.
3. Daddy's heart usually melts when a baby can interact with facial changes, noises, and physical activity like reaching for them or holding on to a finger.
4. Bonding means different things to different people, and babies need all different kinds of bonding.

PART 4

THE FIRST YEAR

"I always say if you can make it through the first two months you are home free."
—*Dr. Cliff James (Hey, it's my book . . . I can quote myself!)*

Istock.com/RichLegg

Why is my baby's poop hard?

That is a good question! It shouldn't be hard.

Why are there so many pages about poop in this book? Well, babies basically eat, sleep, cry, and go to the bathroom. That makes pooping roughly 12.5 percent of the experience (I divided it equally between pee and poop. I know they pee more, but I hate poopy diapers a lot more.) Adjust your expectations accordingly.

If your baby has hard poop, then we call that constipation. Hard stools hurt your baby, and your pediatrician needs to get involved. It could be a temporary thing or possibly more serious. Most urgently, hard

Istock.com/AJ_Watt

stools hurt and no one wants that, so it needs correction.

The question though is, why did it happen?

Most of the time, hard stools will be temporary and will be due to a transition. Let's go through the most common transitions that can lead to constipation.

The first transition will begin somewhere between three and five weeks of age. In this transition, your baby goes from pooping automatically whenever they eat anything to only pooping one or two times per day or even skipping days. As the stooling slows down, waste has more time to hang out in our large intestine and have more water absorbed from it. Absorb enough water and *Boom!* You end up with hard stools.

The second transition could happen if you decide to change which milk your baby is drinking. Probably the most common one we see is if mom decides to stop breastfeeding and go to formula. Formula tries to get close to breast milk, but it is not the same. Because of the change in the size of the proteins, babies will often get constipated during the first week or two. This transition can also happen just going from one formula brand to another,. Even changing the way it is made (i.e., going from ready to feed to powder, even if it's the same type of formula) can have an effect. Your baby is growing and slowly adjusting to new foods as you introduce them.

The third transition we see is when we start adding baby food. Baby food brings a whole new level to digestion. The baby's gut needs to turn something solid into a liquid form and that takes a lot of work and change.

In the beginning, the gut may not be quite up to the challenge. Some foods are more constipating than others, and if those happen to be the baby's favorite, it can lead to the development of some harder stools.

The fourth transition happens when the baby transitions to whole milk. Just like if we changed from breastfeeding to formula or changed formula brands, their little intestinal tract has a hard time transitioning in how it digests the formulation of proteins.

The last transition we see them go through in the baby and toddler stage is as they prepare for potty training. One of the essential parts of being able to potty train is the ability to hold stools. In order to potty train, they need to be able to hold their pee and poop until they can get to the right place to do so. Unfortunately, as they learn to hold their stool, sometimes they can hold it too long and their colon absorbs too much water and leads to constipation.

Finally, you may have a baby that hasn't had a transition at all, but is still constipated. This can be because they have been sick, haven't been drinking enough, or have been losing more fluids through their skin due to hot weather and dry air. Sometimes babies just have a colon that works too well in the process of absorbing water and just makes their stools too hard.

The thing to remember is this: Hard stools hurt! We need to make the stools softer so our baby doesn't have pain every time she goes to the bathroom. You need to call your doctor and find out what to do to help your baby.

What kinds of recommendations will your doctor make? It depends on many things, which is why you need to contact the expert. As poop authorities, we are the #1 source for info on #2. (I know, okay? Sorry. It had to be done.) We will recommend different things depending on how old your baby is, what has led to the constipation, how long it has been going on, and several other factors. Your doctor may wait until the baby has had more than one hard stool to see if it was just a temporary problem due to an illness. They may recommend a simple change in diet. In potty training children, they may recommend a different schedule. They may recommend medication to help your baby go to the bathroom or medicines that make sure the stools stay soft. This is something you really need your doctor to help you sort through to make sure we are doing the best thing for your baby in their specific situation.

The take-home message is that "Why is my baby's stool hard?" is a really good question. It can get complicated, and you need to pose that question to your doctor. The answer they give you will depend on your baby's specific situation.

We love answering poop questions. It's our duty.

Okay, I'll stop now.

TAKE-HOME POINTS:

1. Your baby's poop should not be hard. Hard poop hurts, and we do not want them to hurt.

2. There are a few predictable times when a baby will have transient constipation. We commonly see it happen at one month of age, one year of age when she changes to whole milk, and at two years of age when she starts potty training.

3. If your baby hasn't had a stool in three days and is fussy, crying, or in pain, it is always a good idea to call your doctor.

4. If your baby is always having hard painful stools, then schedule an appointment with your doctor and develop a plan to take care of the problem.

Why should I vaccinate my baby?

Because.

Because why?

Because I said so!

I realize this is a hot-button issue in our society right now. I wish I could somehow wave a wand and make everyone understand the risks and the rewards. I want to be able to just say "trust me" and be done with it and vaccinate everyone. This would be so much easier if I could just pull the parent card on this question and just say, because I said so!

The truth is that you deserve more. You as a parent absolutely deserve to know why you should not only vaccinate your child, but you should demand that he be vaccinated and be passionate about it. You deserve the facts, and you should be able to have reliable info on this subject.

Let's start off with a couple of definitions. The first is "mortality," meaning "death." The second is "morbidity," which means there was a disability. This disability could be the loss of hearing, loss of mental abilities, or loss of physical function. The last would be economic cost, which is how much it costs society due to the illness either in lost work or actual cost to treat the illness.

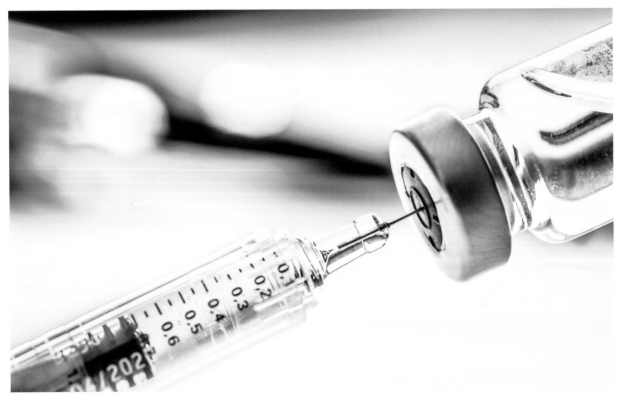

Istock.com/MarianVejcik

The first and most important reason to have a vaccine is if the disease has no cure and has a high chance of causing morbidity and/or mortality. A great example of this was smallpox. There was no cure and it had a death rate of 30 to 35 percent. If you got smallpox you had a 1 in 3 chance of dying. It was a disease that was very contagious. In the 20th century, 300 million people died from smallpox.

Have you noticed I exclusively refer to smallpox in the past tense? That's because the last case of natural smallpox was in 1977. To put that in perspective, now one of the scariest diseases that we are trying to find a vaccine for is the HIV virus. In the last fifty years it has led to the death of 38 million people worldwide. Thankfully, HIV is not as easily transmitted as smallpox was.

Currently we are looking for a vaccine for Covid-19. It also has very little effective treatments and has led to thousands of deaths. It has been a recent reminder of why vaccines are so important in preventing disease, so we can carry on our everyday life.

The second reason to have a vaccine is a significant morbidity following the disease. A great example of this type of disease is Polio. Polio is a virus that typically causes abdominal pain, vomiting, and diarrhea. One out of 1000 children and 1 out of 75 adults that acquired the disease experienced muscle weakness and paralysis. Many of those affected would have their paralysis resolve with time and have a full recovery. In 25 to 50 percent of those afflicted, it would come back ten to twenty years later. This morbidity left many people dependent on crutches, wheelchairs, and even in bed on ventilators. In short, polio was recoverable for most, but those that didn't had very debilitating complications.

The polio virus is on the verge of extinction thanks to vaccine administration that began in the 1950s and a worldwide effort to vaccinate in the 1980s. At the time of this writing, less than 200 cases are known worldwide. Eradication of polio is in sight, and vaccines are the point of the spear in this fight.

The third and final reason to develop and give a vaccine is economics. There is a huge cost to getting sick. We will use chickenpox as an example for this. chicken pox was a common childhood illness before its vaccine usage, and most of us think of it as relatively harmless. Chicken pox parties used to be common. Parents would have infected kids play with uninfected, to "get it over with."

In reality, chicken pox (or Varicella) was not as harmless as thought. In the USA alone, 10,000 to 13,000 children were hospitalized per year and 100 to 200 children died per year. Three to four million cases were reported per year in the United States. The children who acquired chicken pox could be sick and/or infectious for seven to twenty-one days.

To estimate the costs, you have to go beyond treating the disease itself. Look at the costs associated with chicken pox. You might need to miss work to take care of the child, which costs the parent money. Then there are medicines for relief of symptoms like fever and itching. Don't forget there are societal costs for missing school or work too. Teachers spend extra time catching up students who missed time. Your coworkers have to cover the workload while you are out. Then figure in the cost of doctor's appointments for diagnosis and complications. You can keep going down this rabbit hole. It's like throwing a pebble in a pond. The ripples just keep going.

Obviously, we want to prevent all the childhood deaths we possibly can. That said, the main reason for the chicken pox vaccine is economics. When the Centers for Disease Control and Prevention did the economic studies, they found that one dollar invested in the vaccine saved society about five dollars. They then concluded that the chicken pox vaccine was a good economic investment. In addition, the vaccine has almost eliminated severe chicken pox, which results in hospitalization or mortality.

When making decisions about your baby you will often be doing a risk vs. benefit analysis. What is the cost of putting in electric outlet covers and how much of a pain in the neck is it to pull them out all the time vs. how bad is it going to be if my toddler sticks something metal into the outlet? Want to know how often those accidents happened? ALL THE TIME!

That same decision-making comes into play when vaccinating. How bad does the shot hurt, how much does it cost, and what are the side effects of the vaccine? What will the disease cost our family, how sick will it make my child, if my child gets it will they die, and how will that affect you and your family?

Vaccines have been developed over the years to save lives. The vaccine movement is one of the main reasons that pediatrics came into being. Our main job isn't to take care of sick and dying children. Our main job is to prevent illness and dying. We are here to prevent illness and pain, so children grow up to be healthy, happy adults. Vaccination is a primary line of defense against common illnesses.

Your pediatrician would never want to hurt your baby in one way in order to prevent hurting him in another. Science and medicine are constantly trying to improve our outcomes and decrease any side effects or discomfort. We will always be striving to find a better cure or prevention. We are infinitely better at it now than we were 50 years ago. In 50 years, we will be better than we are now.

I will close the book on this with one simple question: Are vaccines the best and safest way to prevent these diseases at this point in time?

The answer is yes, they are.

Could there be another way? Sure, we are always hoping to learn better ways and today more than ever, scientists are striving to make our lives and health better.

TAKE-HOME POINTS:

1. Vaccines are invented to protect us from diseases that either don't have a cure or treatment or that may not be recognized fast enough to prevent death or disability.

2. The reasons for vaccines could be to prevent death, prevent disability, or to decrease the cost of the disease.

3. Vaccines provide a great way to protect your baby, but you deserve to know exactly why they are given so you can make risk vs. benefit decisions regarding your baby.

Why can't my baby have honey?

The year was 1974. I was living in the small town of Elkhart, Kansas. I had a little sister who was suffering from a terrible case of colic. By her suffering, I mean that everyone in the house was suffering from her screaming all the time. I am sure she felt some discomfort, but at the time young me was more concerned with losing my sanity, and perhaps my hearing. The only thing that would make her stop screaming was if she had a pacifier in her mouth. The problem was she didn't want to suck on her pacifier all the time, and if she wasn't sucking on it, she was screaming. The answer came in the form of some old-woman advice—dip the pacifier in honey. That was the ticket. A big wad of honey on the pacifier, and she would suck on that thing like it contained the answers to life itself. The sugar content was probably a factor as well. Suddenly, I had a job in my family. Once the pacifier became sugar deficient, I was in charge of resupply. This is quite possibly the only chore I was ever given that did not require any additional parental motivation. Enthusiastically, I accepted this role and performed it quite well.

Evidently, this advice took off in the South and soon there were a lot of honey-dipped pacifiers saving sanity everywhere. This sounds like a great plan, but it had a terrible flaw. In 1976, the CDC noted a link between honey and a condition they were calling "Floppy Baby Syndrome." These babies would develop sudden weakness of their muscles,

Istock.com/Rawf8

127

paralysis, and even the inability to breathe. Some were dying in their sleep. Upon investigation, the culprit was found to be botulism, a rare form of food poisoning in which the bacteria *Clostridium botulinum* was producing botulinum toxin leading to the symptoms of fussiness, lethargy, muscle weakness, paralysis, respiratory failure, and deaths.

Soon, warnings were all over the news and containers of honey to make sure that people were not giving their babies honey. Unfortunately, warnings have not been enough. Still in Texas to this day, there are eight to ten cases of botulism every year in babies due to honey ingestion. Please, please NEVER give an infant honey. The risks are not worth it.

I guess the next big question would be, why can older children and adults eat honey and not suffer from botulism? The answer has a lot to do with how botulism actually works.

See, honey has a huge concentration of sugar. The sugar content is so high that bacteria can't survive in it. Wait a second, didn't I just say that honey could be contaminated with Clostridium botulinum? The bacteria don't actually live in honey, but botulism spores are often present in it. The spores are kind of like an egg or a seed. The spores can live in the dirt for many years. If given the right environment a single spore can open up and become a fully functioning bacterium. A baby's intestinal tract is that perfect environment.

But why can older children and adults eat honey without any problems? Should I avoid honey?

As we get older, our intestinal secretions become more acidic. This higher level of acid is more likely to destroy the botulism spore. Also, our system is grown and fully developed, while your baby's is still adjusting. Our system processes food fairly quickly, and botulism typically will be processed and headed out as waste before the spore can turn into a functioning bacterium. This tends to happen a little before a child is one year of age.

TAKE-HOME POINTS:

1. Don't give honey in *any* form to your baby until they are at least a year old.
2. See rule #1.
3. If anyone asks, the reason is botulism. If they ask again, show them rule #1.
4. Signs of infant botulism are: fussy, floppy, muscle weakness, respiratory difficulty, and sometimes death.
5. If your baby is exposed to raw honey and shows any of the symptoms please seek immediate medical help.

******I feel the need to mention snacks that are flavored with honey are okay, things like graham crackers that have "flavored with real honey!" written on the box. These are made with honey that has been cooked, and cooking has killed the spores. I know from my homebrewing days that botulism has to be killed by pressure cooking; regular stovetop boiling is not enough. This is why when brewers make starter worts en masse, you pressure cook them for a nice long time.******

Why is my baby crying?

If ever there was one question I could answer and instantly be a gazillionaire, this is the one. I wouldn't even have to have written this whole book. I could have just done this one question, one answer. World's shortest book sells the most copies ever.

Sadly, this is not the case. (At least you got a whole book out of it, so there's that.)

As a pediatrician, I see babies every day because they are crying and the parents don't know why. As a parent, I remember trying to figure out why my baby was crying (oh, and by the way I was already a pediatrician). Trust me, I know that your baby crying can be both frustrating, nerve-racking, and scary all at the same time. Keep in mind nature doesn't make

Istock.com/Korneeva_Kristina

mistakes. Your baby cries at a frequency designed by nature to get your attention. So, if your baby crying gets you a little frazzled and you are worked up about it, all is going according to plan. Isn't that great?

No? Okay, I know it's stressful. I have been in your shoes.

This might seem silly, but we need to address a basic truth of the situation. What kinds of noise can a baby actually make? Not a lot. In the first few months they might make some gurgles, smacks, maybe a coo, but most of the noise that comes out of them will be in the form of a cry. All humans, including babies, have a basic need to communicate. We are social critters. We do not like isolation as a species. So, when your baby wants to express herself, her options are limited. It's kind of like the old adage that if your only tool is a hammer then the whole world looks like a nail. Well, your baby has one tool and it sounds like *WHAAA!! WHAAAAAAAAAAAAA!!!*

Imagine being completely helpless. You can't talk, walk, gesture, or do anything on your own. You are still going to get uncomfortable, bored, hungry, and feel the need to pee and poop, but you can't do anything about any of these things. In order to communicate to get assistance, out comes that vocal hammer. Hopefully a baby can change its cry so that whoever is helping her can figure out what she wants, but that will take a little trial and error on both of your parts. This is a lot for a newborn to process, so give her some time. She will work it out.

In addition to possibly being hungry, wet, tired, lonely, uncomfortable, bored, wanting

to be held, or in pain, she might also be testing to see who her person is.

Wait, testing? What does that testing thing mean?

Go back in time several thousands of years, back when we lived out in the wild and we were prey. It was a wild, savage time. A baby was completely defenseless against the elements and against predators who are looking for a tasty little morsel. That cry could be part of her attempt to find out who the person is that she can depend on to come save her. Sometimes a baby just likes a little reassurance that she has someone who has her back.

The important thing to remember is that there is a reason your baby is crying. It isn't always something bad. As you and your baby learn about each other more, these cries will start to make sense and you will learn what the sound of the cry means. It also doesn't hurt if you learn the baby's schedule. A cry when it has been three hours since she ate last is most likely going to be an "I'm hungry" cry. If you think she is signaling hunger, offer food. When your baby accepts, Congratulations! You have communicated with an infant who cannot speak. You have learned her schedule and hopefully a nuance of the cry itself. You will both get this means of communication down to an art form about the time she learns how to talk, and then you won't need it anymore.

First thing's first. Establish a hierarchy. Why is the baby crying? Keep a mental checklist to run down when it starts.

1. How long has it been since she ate? Could she be hungry again?

2. Is her diaper wet or dirty?

3. How long has it been since she pooped? Could she be crying because she needs to poop and it just hasn't come out yet?

4. Could she be tired? How long has it been since she was asleep or took a nap?

5. Did she eat anything different that might be giving her a bellyache?

6. Is she acting sick? Does she have a fever, a cold, or any increase in stools or spit-up?

7. Will picking her up make her better? It is very rare that picking up a baby that is sick or in pain will make everything better.

Go through the most common list of requests your baby could be trying to make before you get too upset about her crying. If you go through the list and find nothing, and your baby still won't stop crying, then it may be time to enlist some help. Sometimes that help just needs to come in the form of someone else holding the baby and giving you a chance to calm down. Also, keep in mind they're trying to work through this communication thing too. It's possible they are stressed out about it. Maybe they want to tell you something and can't figure out

how. A great method for helping baby with their frustrations is a simple scenery change. Say you're inside with a fussy baby, nothing is working. Hand over baby to another parent or sibling. Have the baby go into another room, or maybe take a walk outside. Sometimes a simple change like that can ease her frustrations, or maybe it just takes her mind off it.

If your baby is not responding to any attempt to soothe, and you have addressed the basics, it may mean that you need to give the baby's doctor a call. Go through the story to see if there is anything that you may need to worry about.

TAKE-HOME POINTS:

1. Babies cry. It's going to happen. It is their only form of communication for several months.

2. Most of the time you can go through a short list and figure out what your baby is trying to tell you.

3. It is a bit nerve-racking at times. Be patient. Don't be afraid to enlist help. Many hands make light work.

4. If your baby will not stop crying and you can't figure it out, then it is time to enlist some help in the form of your doctor.

Why can't I give my child aspirin?

What?

I've never heard that before; who said that?

Don't give your child aspirin! Ever!

There. Now you've heard it.

The only exception would be if your child has a cardiologist or cardiothoracic surgeon telling you to give them aspirin and trust me, they are even a little scared of it.

Why can't I give them aspirin? The label even says "baby aspirin"; how could it be bad for them?

Have you ever heard of a condition called Reye's Syndrome? Don't feel guilty if you haven't. It is a rare condition but can be very serious and even fatal. It has been linked to use of aspirin to treat viral illnesses like chicken pox and influenza. Thanks to the varicella vaccine we don't see chicken pox much anymore, but we still see a lot of the flu. Guess what the flu looks like? It looks like every other cold your child gets. Mostly it causes a fever, headache, lethargy, and a general feeling of malaise. When a child has something that looks like a cold, most parents are going to give their child something for the headache or fever. Things usually take a downturn before the child goes to the doctor and gets the diagnosis of the flu. By the time this happens, the parent has already used aspirin to treat influenza. Therefore, it is easier just to tell parents to avoid aspirin completely.

Why are we so scared of Reye's Syndrome? Well, the symptoms usually show up about five days after the start of the viral illness and include things like vomiting and diarrhea, confusion, seizures, and even death. It affects the liver and causes it to swell and increase fat deposits in the liver. Ammonia levels can rise in the blood and the brain can start to swell. None of these things

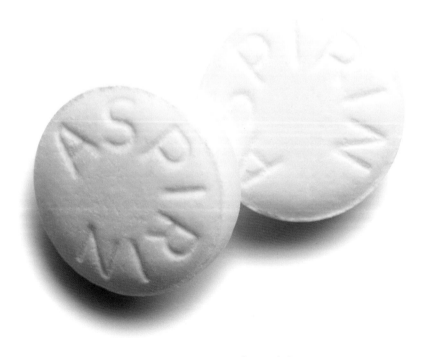

Istock.com/sd619

are great to happen in your child and we want to avoid them at all costs. Unfortunately, there is no specific treatment for Reye's Syndrome. All we can do is make sure the child can breathe, give him fluids, and manage his electrolytes and hydration. Basically, it has to run its course, and we try to manage the symptoms and minimize the permanent damage.

There is also another good reason to avoid aspirin. Aspirin makes the platelets in the blood less effective. This is the reason that people at risk of heart attacks take aspirin daily. Aspirin keeps you from forming clots. It is a type of "blood thinner." Given the fact that kids like to fall, cut, scrape, and generally hurt themselves in various ways, taking away their ability to clot blood is not the greatest idea.

Older folks will sound off a familiar refrain here. "I took aspirin, my friends did too, and we're all fine." Let's keep in mind grandma means well and loves you and the little bundle. Gently remind her that science is always progressing, and we get better every day.

That didn't convince the elders? Fine. Let's talk about Sgt. Alkemade.

Sergeant Nicholas Alkemade was a British pilot in WWII. He was shot down, plane in flames over Germany in 1944. He bailed out at roughly 18,000 feet. One issue—his parachute was on fire and useless. Nicholas decided to jump to his death rather than burn. Only he didn't die.

Yep. Sergeant Nicholas Alkemade fell 18,000 feet in freefall, landed on the ground, and somehow survived. In fact, he had very minor injuries. He was taken prisoner, but once the Germans verified his crazy story, he became a bit of a POW celebrity. He eventually was released in 1945 and went home, supposedly carrying an official document issued to him by the Germans certifying his story.

So, does this mean jumping from a burning airplane at 18,000 feet with no parachute into enemy territory is a safe activity? Of course not, and while the risks are not equal, aspirin isn't safe just because someone survived it. The risks are well-documented, and anecdotal evidence aside, just don't do it.

TAKE-HOME POINTS:

1. Don't give aspirin.
2. If you have to give your child aspirin as directed by a doctor, listen to all the things they tell you to worry about. Follow instructions as given, no winging it.
3. Ignore old people! Don't give your child an aspirin!

Why can't I give my baby cold medicines?

The easy answer is because there aren't any cold medicines for babies. Done.

But WHY?

I'll one up you. Let's not talk about why you can't. Let's look at why there are no baby cold medicines. Huh? Better? I thought so.

The common cold has many symptoms and all of them make babies miserable. The common symptoms of a cold are going to include the following: fever, cough, runny nose, congestion, headache, change in smell,

Istock.com/SDI Productions

change in taste, decreased appetite, and generally just feeling bad.

Think that's awful? Wait, there's more!

In addition to those lovely symptoms, colds can lead to secondary infections like ear infections, sinus infections, and pneumonias. Yayyyyy. It's easy to understand a parent that is left in a panic and just wants it all to go away and go away fast. Unfortunately, it doesn't work that way.

If you talk to older people, you will soon learn that it used to work that way. If you go back twenty years there were lots of products on the market for children to help with their cold symptoms, but there were a few problems. Most of the medicines were using alcohol as their cough suppressant. Studies started to come out on the effects of alcohol on young developing brains and it was no longer recommended to use alcohol in children. The main decongestant being used was a medication called pseudoephedrine. It worked great, but people were using it to manufacture methamphetamine, so it was taken out of most cold medicines. Cold medicine companies were left scrambling to substitute other ingredients to help with the cough and congestion. So, they started using cough suppressants and decongestants that adults were taking, just in smaller doses. Suddenly, there was a huge spike in emergency department visits due to the side effects of these cough medicines in children. An outcry from the pediatric community went up and the Food and Drug Administration stepped in.

The FDA investigated the cough medicine use in children in 2007 and told the drug companies they needed to go back and test all the cough medicines in children to both prove they were safe and that they were more effective than honey was on cough suppression.

So far . . . crickets.

The only cough medicines you are going to find for young children (ages one to four years) are going to be medicines with the main ingredient being honey. Honey can't be used in children less than one year of age, so we are left with no cold medicines for babies.

So, you get to hear from your doctor the thing that parents hate for their pediatrician to tell them. Just try to make them feel better based on their symptoms. In children with a cold, we recommend nasal suction with a bulb syringe and normal saline nose drops or spray and running a vaporizer/humidifier right next to the baby. The bulb suction is trying to remove the obstruction of the nasal mucus. The humidifier is an effort to make the mucus thinner so it doesn't plug up the baby's nose as much and the cough isn't as deep.

Trust me, we understand that you don't like the fact that you can't just give your baby something and make the symptoms go away. But the important thing is to not harm your baby. The symptoms of a common cold are annoying for sure. They are generally not life-threatening, however, and that couldn't be said with absolute certainty about the cold medicines that we were using before.

You are left with trying little things to make your baby or small child feel better. Love on them, feed them, keep them hydrated, and do little things to make them feel better.

Love and affection help you and the baby. It's better than anything at the drugstore.

The common cold usually lasts seven to ten days, and unfortunately your baby/child is going to get a lot of colds in her lifetime. Now armed with this knowledge, you're ready for the task. Show that snot who's boss. Get that bulb thingy out and suck those baby boogers outta there. By the way, clean that thing. THOROUGHLY. It's literally a booger vacuum. Ewwww . . . .

There are some absolute reasons to take your child to the doctor if they have a cold. If they have a fever that lasts longer than three days, it is time to get looked at. If their fever went away for more than 24 hours and then came back, it is time to be examined. If they are having any problems breathing or wheezing, then they need to be seen right now! If they are crying like they are in pain, it is probably a good idea to make sure they haven't developed an ear infection. Finally, if you "feel" like they aren't doing well, or look too sick to you, trust those parental instincts and bring them in to see their doctor.

TAKE-HOME POINTS:

1. Don't give your baby any cold medicines of any kind until he is one year of age.
2. From one to four years of age, you can give medicines that are more homeopathic in nature and use honey as their main ingredient.
3. There are cold medicines that are approved after four years of age. Just know that they aren't effective and you are probably making yourself feel better giving it than you are actually helping your child with their symptoms.
4. ALWAYS call your doctor if your baby seems too sick, gets a fever in the middle or end of a cold, has difficulty breathing, or if you are ever scared or worried about your child.

Why do we wait to introduce solid food to babies?

Sometimes I like to use a little common sense in life. Take a look at your mouth, and then take a look at a newborn's. Notice a glaring difference?

Yes, you have teeth and the newborn doesn't. The reason we hold off on baby food for babies is they are not ready for solid food yet. We will go through all the reasons why to wait, but the baseline answer is they need to wait until they are ready.

Most pediatricians recommend holding off any food except for milk until they are at least four months old, and we would prefer six months. Where I practice pediatrics, it is about all I can do to put them off until four months. Sometimes I can convince them to wait until six months, if I give them good reasons that they can understand.

Why are parents in such a hurry to feed their baby solid foods? I think it comes down to two reasons. The first reason is they believe that eating solid foods will make them sleep longer. Nevertheless, sleeping and eating get paired together more because of timing. Babies start eating baby food between four and six months of age, and most babies start sleeping through the night at four to six months as well. The two are connected by age, but nothing else. Starting baby food early will not help your baby sleep through the night earlier. It's a myth, don't believe it.

The second reason parents want to feed their baby early is because of guilt. We feel guilty that we are eating all this yummy food and all the baby is getting is bland milk, all the time. We take their curious looks and looks of longing and we feel bad and want them to have something else to eat like we do. There you are, scarfing down a delicious helping of biscuits and gravy. Your baby is staring at it. Then at you. Then at it, then you. Clearly this is an effort to communicate a deep, longing need for cholesterol.

However, there are several developments that have to take place before a baby is ready to eat solid food. The first is the ability to hold his head up and to be able to sit upright to eat. Swallowing solid food works best with gravity. If you've ever tried to drink or eat lying down, you know what I'm talking about.

Next, babies need to develop the necessary muscle movements of their tongue to be able to push the food to the roof of their mouth and back in order to swallow it. Babies not ready to eat will push the food to the side and into their cheeks or just straight back out their mouth.

The last thing that needs to develop is gut maturity. A baby's intestines need to mature in the way they absorb food and push it through. The absorption is important in order to get nutrients from the food, filter out harmful substances, and be able to process

Istock.com/RuslanDashinsky

proteins in a way that keeps us from developing food allergies. The intestines also need to be able to push through the digesting and undigested food in order to have normal bowel movements.

You also have to consider the specifics of your baby:

- If you have a baby who has already had problems with an allergy to milk, or had eczema or asthma problems, pediatricians absolutely recommend waiting until they are six months of age to try solid food.

- If you have a strong family history of eczema, asthma, or food allergies, most pediatricians will recommend waiting until six months of age.

- If your baby was born premature or has had any problems swallowing milk or a history of aspirations, you need to consult with your pediatrician as to when and how to introduce solid foods.

Once you do introduce solid food, there's the question of which foods to try. If you were to ask 100 pediatricians how to introduce baby food, you would probably get 100 different answers and most of them could be correct. I will leave it up to your doctor to help you through the maze of baby food. I think the one thing we can agree on is that rice cereal is bad. It is commonly used to teach babies how to use a spoon, but it has no nutritional component to it at all. It has the benefit of being cheap, mostly hypoallergenic, and you can play with the consistency and texture a little. As soon as your baby can swallow, I really think you should stop the rice cereal, go to baby food, and never give rice cereal again. This will vary baby to baby and could be just a few days or a few weeks before they get the hang of using a spoon.

Remember, the perfect food for your young baby is breast milk. The closest we have gotten to breast milk is formula, and for the first half of their first year that is all they need. Their milk gives them the perfect number of calories, protein, fat, and nutrients that their growing bodies need. Solid food can't duplicate that.

TAKE-HOME POINTS:

1. Do not introduce solid food to your baby until he is four to six months of age. Waiting until six months is best.
2. If you have a baby who has had a food allergy, asthma, or eczema, wait until six months of age to introduce solid foods.
3. If you have a family history of food allergies, asthma, or eczema, wait until six months of age to introduce solid foods.
4. If your baby was born premature or has any swallowing difficulty, consult your pediatrician before introducing solid foods.
5. Ask your pediatrician how they recommend introducing solid foods to your baby as well as how much and how frequently the baby needs to eat.

Why does my baby scream when I leave the room?

Chances are that if you are asking this question, your baby is one of two ages. They are either a very little baby (less than two months of age) or they are between 9-15 months old. In both cases, it is very normal and there is nothing wrong with your baby.

Let's start off with the first stage, the first two months of life. We covered this same topic in another "Why" question about crying. Babies have instincts to keep them safe. A little baby always wants to be near someone. Babies know they are helpless and they

Istock.com/mdphoto16

would like a bodyguard to keep them safe. If you are leaving the room, then they have lost their bodyguard. Additionally, they really like to be warm and snuggly and the best way is by being right next to you. If you leave the room, their warm and snuggly has left.

If you are breastfeeding your baby then they know your smell. You are the smell of food and happiness. As you get farther away, food and happiness are leaving and taking warmth and protection with it. (Geez, that sounds bleak, doesn't it?)

The important thing to understand about this stage of life is that it is very normal. You are not spoiling your baby by being close to him. In fact, you are giving him exactly what he needs. It doesn't mean he is spoiled if he cries when you leave, either. In the first couple of months, don't hesitate to keep the little bundle right with you as much as possible. It's good for both of you.

As he starts to become more independent and secure in his environment he won't get so upset when you leave the room. They get where they can see what is going on, and they can find things around them to keep their interest. They begin to entertain themselves and they can go longer periods of time in between meals. At around two months of age for most babies they let their moms have a little longer leash. It won't last; enjoy it while you can.

The second time we will see the baby getting upset when you leave the room will start somewhere around nine to twelve months of age. This is when a baby starts to develop separation anxiety. Many parents worry that they have done something that has led their baby to feel less secure. Other parents worry that something has happened to their baby and they are now scared due to that memory. Neither of those are likely. This is just a normal developmental state that a baby goes through. In this stage of life if you leave their sight then you have left their world. In their eyes, they are still very vulnerable and if alone they are in trouble. When they see that you are not around, they will completely lose their mind. In a cruel twist of fate, their lungs are also more developed, and they have better stamina. They are like custom-built super-charged crying machines.

Many parents during this stage find it hard to even go to the bathroom by themselves and end up just taking a baby with them to avoid the screaming fit. The important thing to remember is this will pass. A piece of your sanity will pass with it. There's no sense worrying about their crying or your sanity, nothing can be done about either one.

Of course, every baby is different. There will be babies who will start early, and some will start late. Some parents will get lucky and will never see much of this at all. Some babies will do this for a year or more. Just remember that your baby is normal and you are not scarring them for life. Babies cry; it's just about all they have for communication.

To try and ease your baby's anxiety (and your own), there are a couple of things you can do. Make sure you are always talking to your baby and he knows where you are. Don't just suddenly disappear; tell him you are going and exactly where. Continue to talk to him when you are in the other room. This will start to condition him that even when you can't be seen you are still there and can be contacted. If your baby gets upset, don't just let him scream; talk to him and get back to him fairly quickly. If he just gets left alone then his fears have merit. The more secure he feels in his environment and in his relationship with you, the shorter amount of time you will be dealing with separation anxiety.

Now there are children that suffer from worse separation anxiety and have problems being left anywhere. They have a hard time going to school or daycare. This can continue in later childhood and even adulthood, which is a much bigger subject not well suited to this book. Your pediatrician may be able to help; talk to them if this is happening to your child.

TAKE-HOME POINTS:

1. Your newborn screaming when you leave the room is not a sign that he is spoiled. It is more an instinctual worry about survival.

2. Responding to your newborn screaming is not spoiling your baby; it is called parenting.

3. Your nine- to twelve-month-old screaming when you leaving the room is normal separation anxiety and is not your fault. It is a normal developmental stage.

4. There are things you can do to decrease the amount of time that your baby has separation anxiety, but don't expect a quick overnight fix. You may decrease it to two months instead of four.

5. If your child's separation anxiety lasts past the time they are two years old, it is time to talk to your pediatrician.

Why won't my baby sleep through the night?

Talk about a million-dollar question. If I could get all babies to magically sleep through the night as soon as they were born, I would be rich beyond my wildest dreams. I might even qualify for sainthood. I bet I could get knighted, and I'm not even British. It's that big a deal.

Unfortunately, I don't have that multi-bazillion-dollar answer, but I do have some answers as to why it is not happening.

I know it's not as good. I'm not holding out on you, I promise. My kid woke up at 3 a.m. too.

To best answer this question, we kind of need to divide babies into three groups. These correspond to different ages, but I'm going to refer to them as the "can't," "don't know how," and "don't want to" groups. I just like to mix things up every once in a bit to keep it fresh!

Istock.com/Artfoliophoto

Let's start with the "can't" group. This is a truly desperate parental group. These are the babies who are less than two months of age. These parents face the world with one bleary eye open, begging for the sweet release of REM sleep. Well, I have to tell you something, and you aren't going to like it.

This group of babies really can't sleep through the night and they really aren't supposed to.

When I say that, I mean it is really not good for them to sleep all night long. For 22 years I have listened to parents ask how to get them to sleep and tell me all the ways they have tried and all the advice they have been given on how to get them to sleep through the night.

Stop! Pump those brakes, and welcome to parenthood! If you didn't know that you were going to lose some sleep when you decided to have a baby, you didn't do much research.

Very young babies have a storage problem. They can't drink enough at a time, nor can they store enough energy to make it more than about three to four hours before they need to eat again. If they are sleeping through the night, it usually means they are too weak to wake themselves up. That is not good. There is not an exact age where it is fine for a baby to sleep through the night and there will be that rare baby that can get to this point by the time she is six weeks old, but most will be over two months old before they can sleep through the entire night. Don't do anything to try and make it happen. Don't try any folk wisdom, wives' tales, magical elixirs, or any other form of hoodoo to make them

sleep longer. They actually NEED to eat that often. They NEED to wake up. Consequently, you NEED to suck it up and deal with it. Sorry folks, it is what it is.

The next group we will call the "don't know how to" babies. These are the babies that are over two months of age and technically could sleep through the night, but they just don't know how. This is when all that sleep training stuff you have read and heard about can start happening. Whatever it is called by the latest guru, it is a way of teaching your baby how to sleep through the night and giving the proper environment to make it happen. The best piece of advice I can give you is schedule. The second piece of advice I would give you is stick to the schedule. The third piece of advice I would give is never vary from the schedule. What is this magical schedule? Schedule everything, yes everything. Babies do best if nothing varies. Their bath time should be the same, their nap time should be the same, they should eat at the same time, go to bed at the same time, and even wake up at exactly the same time. The more scheduled their life is the more likely they are to sleep through the night. As far as all the other methods to get a baby to sleep through the night I will let you check out all the gurus' books and you can pick your favorite method. For most of you, just heeding the advice of scheduling everything will get your baby to sleep through the night.

The last group I refer to as the "don't want to" group. I personally think these babies hate their parents and are intent on overthrowing the family government through the torture process known as sleep deprivation.

Unfortunately for the parents, this process is very effective. You see these parents looking like they escaped a natural disaster, yet are somehow intact. Shoes may not match, and they may be three hours into their day before they realize they are grocery shopping in a robe and fuzzy slippers. It seems they not so much left the house as survived it, yet for some reason have chosen to bring their tor-menter with them, and in fact lovingly care for the instrument of their destruction. If you see these poor parents out in the wild you may offer support. Do not, and I repeat *do not* attempt to give these people advice. They don't want it. If you truly want to help them, watch the baby while they are enclosed in a soundproof room with a bed.

These babies seem just fine only sleeping two to three hours at a time with multiple long breaks in between. These are the babies who proliferate the gurus that make the money selling books to desperate parents.

I will apologize right now for my lack of great advice. I'm not sure that one method works better than another for these kids. My theory is that parents will try one method after another and the only reason that one method works is because at that exact moment in time their baby decided they wanted to sleep. Their parents become a disciple of that method and look to convert other desperate parents. Maybe this is how the gurus are born.

Even with these babies my best advice is schedule, schedule, schedule. They will fight every step of the way, but eventually it will work, and you will get some sleep.

TAKE-HOME POINTS:

1. It is completely normal for your baby to not sleep through the night. If your newborn is sleeping through the night, talk to your doctor and make sure the baby is okay.
2. After two months of age, babies can start to sleep through the night. Babies are not all the same, and it will happen at different times for different babies. Try and make your schedule the same every day and it will happen for most babies.
3. The babies that just refuse to sleep through the night may stay that way. My advice is still stick to a schedule. Also, this is maybe when you want to check out a book on baby sleep by one of the experts. Or ask Grandma if she would consider coming over more often.

Why does my six-month-old look orange?

I guess the question could be, "Why does my baby look like they have a fake tan?" Anyway, if your baby is a funny pumpkin color of yellowish-orange and is no longer a newborn possibly subject to neonatal jaundice, what is it?

I am going to put in my protect-the-baby-first statement here.

Go see your baby's doctor. Chances are this is nothing to worry about and I'm going to explain the most likely reason below. Anytime your baby has a color change and you notice it, you should just run it by your doctor. The reason for the doctor visit is to rule out any jaundice. Even though we are past the newborn stage when we see jaundice frequently, jaundice can still happen in older babies and children. Jaundice in a six-month or older child is much scarier than the jaundice we see in the newborn period. It would

Istock.com/ManoAfrica

146

usually indicate a problem with the liver and could range from some sort of obstruction to an infection. DON'T PANIC; it is very likely the benign item we're going to discuss in a few sentences. I just want a doctor to see what is going on and verify it is no big deal.

Okay, now what is the most likely cause of your baby looking like they have just got out of the spray tan booth?

Carotenosis.

Answered all your questions, didn't it?

I'm not a fan of big words either. We need to trudge through a couple more ten-penny words to understand the answer here, so bear with me. Carotenosis is caused by the excessive ingestion of carotenoids. I swear, I am not making that up.

The explanation is about as clear as the diagnosis. Here's the simplified version. Carotenoids are the substances that give vegetables their yellow, orange, and red colors. When we eat too many of these veggies, then they accumulate in the skin and give it a funny yellow or orange color. It is completely harmless and will go away as soon as they stop eating as many of these vegetables.

You may be asking yourself how did this happen? We usually begin to see this when you start to give your baby the Stage 2 and Stage 3 baby foods. You will notice that Stage 1 baby foods were all single-entity foods. Stage 2 and Stage 3 baby foods tend to be blends to give them a little more variety of taste. Also, it is done to introduce foods that babies may not like on their own. How do we make a food taste better to a baby? Add sugar! Now we don't want to just pour some table sugar into our baby's food, so we add natural sugars from sweeter foods. Things like carrots and sweet potatoes have a lot of natural sugar in them and they can hide the taste of food that a baby might not enjoy as much.

Now go back and look at all your baby food jars. Even though you are mixing up the types of food you are giving your baby, you will find they are getting several helpings of orange and yellow vegetables. Don't worry, they are good for your baby. They are also what is responsible for that funny-looking tan that they have acquired. Soon enough your baby will be on table foods and eating the same foods that you prepare for the rest of your family on a daily basis. There is a good chance you don't eat orange and yellow vegetables at every meal and the yellow color of your baby will soon fade into just a memory.

> ## TAKE-HOME POINTS:
>
> 1. If your baby is looking a different color, go see your doctor. Every time.
> 2. See rule #1.
> 3. Most likely the yellow-orange color is due to the excessive ingestion of carotenoids (yellow and orange vegetables).
> 4. If #3 is true, the color causes no problems besides acting as a conversation starter and will go away as they eat less orange and yellow vegetables.

Why do babies need tummy time?

This is one of those questions that just seems to beg for the what, when, why, and how kind of answer. Since it seems to beg for it, that is exactly how I will answer it!

What is tummy time? It's exactly what it sounds like—time spent on your tummy. This may be lying on the tummy against the parent's chest or abdomen. This is often thought of as the baby laying on her tummy on the floor. Well, it eventually will be; it is kind of a progression positioning thing. As a newborn, it will be the baby against you on your chest and shoulder while you are standing, reclining, or laying down. As the

Istock.com/NiseriN

baby starts to develop a little head control by a month of age, she should be laying on your chest and abdomen while you are laying down. You interact with her by making eye contact, touching her, and talking with her at this stage. As she develops good head control and stronger neck muscles around two months of age, she can do more tummy time on the floor or a flat surface.

When should tummy time happen? As previously mentioned, it starts pretty much at birth with just the normal type of holding and interacting with your baby and progresses around the time she is two months of age. I usually start to recommend "tummy time" to parents at the two-month check-up and suggest that we aim for two 10-minute intervals during the day. This time period will increase as she gets better at holding her head up and learns to interact with her environment. This is something that is best felt out individually for your baby. Some babies in the beginning just hate it, and that 10 minutes seems like an eternity. Other babies really seem to like the control they have, and how they can look around and interact with their environment. As your baby tolerates and even enjoys it more, she should get to spend more time on her belly. Between four and six months old, she is going to learn to roll over well. Then tummy time is something she can enjoy whenever and for however long she chooses.

There's also the question of time of day. Use some good common sense when giving your baby tummy time. Think about when you would not want to lay on your belly. Tummy time isn't for right after the baby drank her milk or ate her food. If she didn't burp well, it

might not be time to get on their belly. When you are rushing around and don't have time to interact with them, it isn't the right time for tummy time (at least not when she is really young). Make sure the timing is right to ensure a good time is had by all.

Why do babies need tummy time? There are several different reasons. The first pertains to the shape of their head. Babies these days tend to have flatter heads in the back because we recommend that they sleep on their backs all the time. Tummy time gives the back of their head a break. As they grow and their mobility increases, they can change the positioning of their head while they sleep, and their head gets more chances to round back out.

It is also important because it offers babies the opportunity to have different views of their world. When she is on her belly she can look down, straight ahead, to the sides, and up. Suddenly, the world got bigger and the thought of new possibilities begins. It also allows her to build up the muscles in her neck, arms, shoulders, and chest that will eventually be needed to learn to roll over, sit up, and crawl. There is a certain amount of independence that she gains when she is in charge while on her belly, and this will spur her on to the next steps of development.

How does tummy time need to happen? The answer should be in a variety of ways. In the beginning it is just a bonding time wherein the baby is spending time next to her caregivers. After two months of age it needs to be more of a "thing" that is planned. Tummy time shouldn't just be alone time on the floor. That is a great reason for a baby to be upset. Want to make a baby cry? Leave them alone on the floor, feeling stuck, bored, and abandoned. This should be a time of interaction and exploring for the baby. You need to get on the floor with them. Have interesting things down there for them to look at, interact with, and touch. In the beginning, all the interactions will need to happen with your help. You will need to do things with specific toys to grab their attention. You will need to put things against their face and hands so they can touch different textures. You will need to play with toys and show how they move, work, or make noise. This is a great bonding time for you and your baby. As they get older and more in control of their environment, it can become a time of more independent play and exploration. This will come with time. Just watch your baby for clues of when she is ready to move to the next stage.

TAKE-HOME POINTS:

1. Tummy time is important and starts in some ways right after your baby is born.
2. Around two months of age is when pediatricians recommend that tummy time be an actual activity that happens on the floor or a flat surface.
3. Make sure this is a pleasant time for your baby. Plan to have a comfortable place on which to lay down, time to interact with your baby, and interesting things to interact with such as different textures, noise makers, or toys.
4. Make sure you enjoy the time as well. If you aren't having fun, there may be a reason your baby doesn't like it either.

Why does my baby keep getting a cold?

This has to be one of the more frustrating things for parents. It is January and my baby has had eight colds in the last three months. It has seemed like he is sick more than he is well. We just get him better and then a couple of days later he is sick again. Is there something wrong with his immune system? Does he need to be worked up for an immunodeficiency? Do we need to give him vitamins? What is going on?

Istock.com/RyanJLane

Oh, and by the way, as a parent I am mad at you as our pediatrician because every time I bring him to the office you tell me it's a cold and there isn't anything to do for him and he just keeps getting sick. I'm demanding that you do something—give him some antibiotics or order some bloodwork, recommend a vitamin or supplement or something. I want him better and I want him to stay well.

If you have never thought the above conversation, or actually had it with your pediatrician, it is only because your baby is too young, they haven't been through a winter sick season yet, or your baby lives in a bubble. It is so frustrating as a parent to watch your baby get sick over and over again and not be able to do anything to make him better, especially when it doesn't seem like the doctors have anything to help either. It is a little maddening.

Let's start with the culprits that cause the common cold. The common cold (in medical terms called a URI, upper respiratory tract infection) is caused by several families of viruses that include: rhinoviruses, coronaviruses, respiratory syncytial virus, and parainfluenza. There is estimated to be between two hundred and three hundred viruses in these families that cause common cold symptoms. They tend to invade through the respiratory tract and are spread via respiratory droplets. They enter the body through the eyes, nose, or mouth; take up shop in our own cells; and turn our own cells into factories to make more copies of themselves so they can go out into the world and infect more people and make more copies.

In the process of them setting up shop to make more copies of themselves, we as humans feel very sick. Some of the symptoms we feel are due to the virus and what it is causing, but other symptoms are due to our body's response to the viral invasion and trying to kill the viruses. Symptoms like runny nose, headache, and cough would be caused by the virus because this is how it will spread to other people. On the other hand, a symptom like fever is caused by our own body mounting a defense against the virus and trying to kill it and remove it from our body.

Symptoms of the common cold include: fever, cough, congestion, runny nose, headache, sneezing, fatigue, and some slight aches and pains. These come in a fairly predictable order. We usually see fever in the very beginning and then congestion, headache, and sore throat. Cough comes next and continues to get worse, peaking at about day three to six. Most cold symptoms will last about seven to fourteen days. Along the course of the cold it can cause other problems like raw nose, chapped lips, and chest pain from all the coughing.

It is not unusual for a common cold to lead to what we in the medical field call a secondary infection. These are infections like: ear infections, sinus infections, or pneumonia and typically happen in the middle to the end of a cold. These are usually caused by bacteria that normally live in our nose and throat, but then end up somewhere they shouldn't be and set up shop and cause an infection. Normally our body defenses would prevent these, but they let down their guard while fighting off the cold virus and the bacteria takes advantage of our body's moment of weakness. Now unlike a virus, a bacterial infection is treated with antibiotics.

The way our immune system works is through memory. Once we get a cold virus and learn how to fight it off, we will develop antibodies to that virus. These antibodies provide the memory of the virus and how to kill it. If we are exposed to the virus again, we will either not get it at all or be able to fight it off very quickly. The problem lies in the fact that we have to get the virus in order to develop memory to fight it off. The only other way to develop memory is via immunizations. Immunizations provide a way to give our body a fake illness so it learns how to fight it off without actually getting the illness. This is especially important with viruses that have a high chance of causing significant harm, illness, or death before our body can fight it off.

Remember in the beginning when I said there were hundreds of viruses that cause the common cold? That is the reason your baby keeps getting a cold. They have to get a bunch of them before they are going to have a significant memory bank of antibodies to fight them off. The typical baby is going to get seven to ten colds per year. If a cold lasts seven to fourteen days at a time, it is easy to see that your baby may have a cold seventy to a hundred days out of the year. You should also notice that every time your baby gets a cold, you don't always get it from them. That is because in your life at some time you already had that cold and are now immune. As your baby gets older, he will get fewer colds, because his bank of remembered viruses continues to grow.

There is nothing you can give your baby to prevent a common cold. Vitamins like vitamin C have a role in fighting illnesses but will not prevent a cold. Keeping your baby from getting his hair wet outside or covering his head will not prevent a cold. The only way of protecting your baby from cold viruses is by avoiding places with high concentrations of viruses (daycares, shopping, church), practicing good handwashing, and cleaning surfaces that your baby touches frequently.

TAKE-HOME POINTS:

1. The common cold is not caused by a virus, but rather hundreds of different viruses.
2. Your baby is not getting the same cold over and over, but rather different colds that have similar symptoms.
3. It is normal for a child to get seven to ten colds per year.
4. Antibiotics will not help with viruses because they only help with bacteria.
5. Good handwashing and hygiene go a long way in preventing infections with a cold.

Why does my child get ear infections?

Well, there are a bunch of reasons why your child might get ear infections, but it's important to understand the ear before we can explain why. For simplicity sake, we are going to divide the ear into three parts: the outer ear (the part you could see), the middle ear (where the ear infection occurs), and the inner ear (where the action of hearing and balance take place).

For the purpose of this subject we are only going to pay attention to the middle ear. The middle ear has the eardrum. By the way, the eardrum is waterproof; you can't get an ear infection by water getting into your ear. Also, in the middle ear is an air-filled space that contains the three smallest bones of the body. Those tiny bones assist greatly with the conversion of sound waves and make hearing possible. Those sound waves from the outer ear turn into the electrical stimuli that leaves the inner ear. It is in this air-filled space that an infection occurs. The middle ear connects to the throat through a tube called the eustachian tube. This tube goes from the middle ear to the throat between the adenoids and the tonsils. That eustachian tube is the culprit causing the ear infection. If anything causes the tube to become blocked, a vacuum occurs in the middle ear and the path to an infection begins. What happens is that when a vacuum occurs in the middle ear, it pulls fluid into the normally air-filled space. Finally, bacteria from the nose and throat find a way up the canal and into that fluid that the bacteria see as food, and *Bam!* we have an ear infection.

So, why does it happen?

First, something has to block the eustachian tube. The tube is lined with the same kind of skin lining the inside of our nose and throat. Therefore, anything that can make your nose swell shut can make the tube swell shut as well. All the same things that irritate your nose and throat like allergens, dust,

Istock.com/sdominick

tobacco smoke, etc. have the same effect on the eustachian tube. The fact that a child's eustachian tube is much smaller makes it easier to swell shut. What an adult may feel as a slight puffy nose can be a restricted tube in a little one. The smaller the child, the smaller the eustachian tube. Swollen tonsils or adenoids can pinch the opening of the tube closed and cause an obstruction. The smaller the child the more colds they get per year, which comes with increased infection risk.

Dang doc, you got any good news? This is none too promising so far.

Sorry, we're not done yet.

Some other things that can cause swelling would include irritants like perfumes, cigarette smoke, mucus obstruction due to teething . . . you get the idea. Can family history cause problems? Sure, the eustachian tube can run smaller in some families. Sometimes it can have odd bends in it that are hereditary. Also, smoking tends to happen more in certain families than others.

Can you prevent an ear infection?

Well, sorry, but no. Not really. You can avoid risky behavior and try to limit infections. Keep your baby away from tobacco smoke, and try to keep your child away from sick people. That is about all you can do. If you see frequent ear infections, it might be time to examine your exposures to common irritants. It may also be time to consider allergies or even an immune problem being the cause. We may also have to think about putting in a set of PE (pressure equalizing) tubes. This is to prevent that vacuum from occurring in the middle ear. Removing the tonsils or adenoids if they are blocking the eustachian tube is also an option.

PE tubes are a temporary fix, trying to keep the pressure equal on both sides of the eardrum and to prevent a vacuum from developing behind the eardrum. Without that vacuum, fluid can't build up in the space. Without the fluid, an ear infection has less of a chance of developing. (Notice I didn't say "won't develop," I said "less chance." Ear infections are pretty much inevitable.)

The tubes will usually last less than two years. The hope is that in that time your child will grow and it will be harder for the eustachian tube to swell shut. As the tube gets larger and closer to adult size, ear infections are less likely. This is why they're not common in adults.

TAKE-HOME POINTS:

1. Smaller children have a higher chance of getting ear infections due to the fact that the eustachian tube is smaller and therefore easier to swell shut and form the vacuum required to set up an infection.
2. Smaller children tend to get colds more often and have more opportunities to develop an ear infection.
3. If you feel that your child is having too many ear infections, it may be time to discuss his exposure to irritants or PE tubes to help prevent ear infections in the future.

Why does my baby pull on her ear?

I get to see babies all the time who are in my office for pulling on their ear. Because parents can't see the inside of baby's ear, they worry that it might be because of an ear infection. There are several reasons why a baby might be pulling on their ear. They range from cute, to of mild concern, to something we need to worry about. Kind of leaves parents in a pickle, doesn't it? Luckily, there are some ways to figure out whether or not you need to be worried or see a doctor for it.

There are several structures in very close proximity to the ear. Whenever there are lots of nerves crammed very close together, our

Istock.com/ FYMStudio

brain has a hard time telling exactly where the pain is coming from. So, it's already challenging, and if you have a baby who may not even say "dada" yet trying to tell you where the pain is coming from, it's even more challenging.

When I was in medical school, one of my instructors taught me the rule of "T." He said to think of all the things in the area around the ear that start with the letter "T," and remember those could all lead to ear pain. So, what are all the things that start with "T"? They include the outer "tube" canal of the ear, the tympanic membrane (the ear drum), the eustachian "tube," the tonsils, the tongue, the teeth, the throat, and the templar-mandibular joint. True enough, throughout the years, I have seen kiddos in my office complaining of ear pain for reasons that relate to all the different "T"s.

Let's start with the elephant in the room, the tympanic membrane. This is where your classic ear infection occurs. The tympanic membrane is commonly known as the eardrum and when your child's doctor is looking into the ear, he or she is looking at the tympanic membrane. An ear infection will show up with a tympanic membrane that is red, bulging, and has fluid or pus behind it. Sometimes it can have a hole through it. There will be blood or pus leaking through the hole. This is what parents think of every time kids are pulling at their ears, or complain of ear pain. Here is a good rule of thumb. Most infections of the middle ear will happen at the middle or end of a cold or while the child is suffering from allergies. If your child hasn't had nasal congestion or a runny nose for a few days, you are probably not dealing with an ear infection. I wouldn't claim that this is 100 percent accurate, but it has to be at least 98.5 percent of the time. If your child has had a cold or allergies and starts pulling on the ear or crying with ear pain, a visit to the doctor is warranted.

The next most common reason a baby will pull on their ears is teething. The nerves that go to the gums pass right next to the ear. This is called referred pain. I like to explain it in terms of your funny bone. If you've ever hit your elbow just right, a shooting pain will go into your fingers. You didn't do anything to your fingers, but they sure hurt like you did. The same thing happens with teething. The pain is happening at the baby's gums, but she is feeling ear pain. This can be figured out because she hasn't had a cold or allergies and she is obviously teething. If they are pulling on their ears as well, it is most likely referred pain.

In the slightly bigger kids, we will often have them come in complaining of ear pain due to strep throat. (Again, those tonsils start with "T" and they are very close to the eardrum.) They are often sick with fever and they are usually coming to the doctor because they are sick. Their parents are just surprised by the diagnosis, because they thought for sure it had to be an ear infection.

In the summer, we will see children with excruciating ear pain that is due to an infection of the outer canal of the ear. This is often caused by "swimmer's ear," which is an infection of the skin that covers the canal. It occurs in kids who swim frequently, washing all the wax out of the ear canal and leaving it dry. When the skin gets dry it cracks, which allows bacteria from the water to get through the defenses of the skin and cause a skin infection. These kids rarely pull on their ear because that makes it hurt worse! They are crying in severe pain and need some relief. This is usually treated with topical antibiotics.

The eustachian tube is the connecting tube from the middle ear to the throat. This is what keeps the pressure behind the eardrum the same as the pressure outside. If the eustachian tube gets blocked from swelling due to a cold or allergies, it allows a vacuum to develop behind the eardrum. This vacuum can cause pain, or it can lead to the middle ear filling up with fluid. This is very often the precursor to an ear infection. Sometimes kids feel the pressure and will pull on their ear, trying to get their ears to pop.

We will also see kids with sores on their tongue. Yep, crazy as it sounds, it can happen. These kids are sick with something and complaining of ear pain. When the doctors take a look, they will find that the location causing the pain is actually the tongue. This is probably the least common cause of ear pain in the pediatric population, but it does happen with illnesses like hand-foot-mouth disease and lesions like canker sores.

The final "T" is the pain caused by TMJ. TMJ is the inflammation of the templar-mandibular joint. In kids, this can be caused by malalignment of teeth as they are coming in or if you have a child that is going to need braces. It can also be caused by overuse due to grinding their teeth, chewing gum, or constantly consuming chewy substances. It usually presents with the story of ear pain that is worse whenever they are talking, yawning, or eating. Most of time it can be treated with just some avoidance of the chewing, some anti-inflammatories, or in extreme cases bite blocks or braces.

TAKE-HOME POINTS:

1. There are lots of reasons that your child could be pulling on their ear or having ear pain; don't just jump to ear infection.
2. If your child is sick and complaining of ear pain, by all means go to the doctor.
3. If your child is screaming or in terrible pain, go to the doctor and figure out the cause of the pain.
4. If your baby is just pulling on their ear and hasn't been sick and isn't crying, it is okay to just watch until something gets worse.

Why did my child get pneumonia?

This little write-up could have easily been titled, "How did my child get pneumonia?" or probably what most parents want to know, "Is it my fault that my child got pneumonia?" Let me just jump to the chase and let you know that it is not your fault that your baby got pneumonia. As parents we try to take too much credit for the bad things that happen to our children. This one is not your fault. I guess I could imagine how you could give your child pneumonia, but if you did that you are a bad person and you probably know it. If you are worried that you did it . . . you didn't.

A good place to start is what is pneumonia? Pneumonia is an infection of the lungs. More precisely it is an infection of the little air sacs in the lungs called alveoli. This is the place in the lungs where oxygen exchange takes place. We breathe in air and oxygen

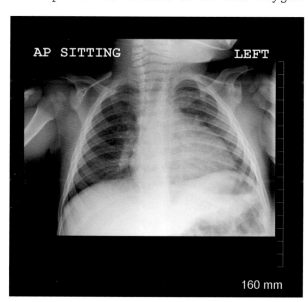

Istock.com/ UrsaHoogle

goes into the body and we get rid of carbon dioxide as we breathe out. It's a little more complicated than that in real life, but for this discussion that works. In these little air sacs, fluid or pus start to accumulate and then we have what we call pneumonia.

Pneumonia can be caused by viruses, bacteria, and occasionally fungal infections in immunocompromised individuals. These infect the air sacs of the lungs and then cause the symptoms and signs that we know as pneumonia.

Symptoms that make you worry that it might be pneumonia can vary from person to person. One of the big worries for me as a physician is a fever that begins in the middle to the end of a cold. A normal cold virus or the flu will have a fever the first two to three days, but once it is gone it shouldn't come back. A fever that pops up in the middle to end of a cold has me worried about secondary infections like the flu. Other symptoms that make you worry is a cough that changes and becomes more productive. Complaints or signs that your child has chest pain, shortness of breath, or difficulty breathing are also symptoms that should send up warning signs. Sometimes they will complain of abdominal pain and even have nausea and vomiting when getting pneumonia.

So how did the pneumonia happen? In the case of viral pneumonias, they are usually contagious. Viruses that cause colds, influenza, and RSV are all capable of causing pneumonia and your child got these from a child or adult that had the virus and was contagious. Most of the bacterial causes of pneumonia are called secondary infections. These bacteria normally reside in our nose and throat and when our body gets weak fighting some other infection or due to body stressor, they take the opportunity to cause an infection. In the case of the fungal pneumonias, these happen in very sick children with AIDS, cancer, severely premature babies, and children in intensive care for other reasons.

What can you do to prevent pneumonia? Well, in the case of viral pneumonia you would prevent it the way you would prevent any cold. Good handwashing goes a long way. Teaching your child to cover his mouth with his elbow when he coughs or sneezes. Teaching your child to not touch his eyes or put his hands in his mouth, and just trying to avoid sick people during the height of cold season. In the cases of bacterial pneumonia, make sure your baby is up to date on all his vaccines. Bacteria like Strep pneumonia and H. flu are covered by the normal childhood vaccines. For the other bacterial pneumonias, make sure your child is getting plenty of rest and fluids when he is sick, and watch carefully while he is sick for any signs of pneumonia so you can get it diagnosed quickly. With fungal infections you are usually dependent upon hospitals and doctors to try to minimize the risk in your child who is already vulnerable and very sick.

Treatments for pneumonia depend on the cause. If the pneumonia is caused by bacteria, your doctor will prescribe antibiotics. Pneumonias caused by viruses just need symptomatic treatment. Fungal pneumonias are very serious and will be treated in the hospital, usually with anti-fungal agents. Just remember, pneumonia is a very serious illness. Follow your doctor's recommendations and if your child is not getting better or is getting worse let your doctor know immediately.

TAKE-HOME POINTS:

1. Pneumonia is not your fault!
2. You can prevent some pneumonias by making sure your child's vaccines are all up to date.
3. Good handwashing, hygiene, and Lysol go a long way in helping to prevent pneumonia.
4. Don't underestimate the good care you give while your child is sick. Making sure they are getting good rest, staying hydrated, and loving on them does more than you think.
5. Always go to your doctor if you suspect your child has pneumonia.

Why do antibiotics cause diarrhea?

Let's just start off by saying that all medicines have side effects. Whenever a doctor decides to write a prescription for anything, the first question he should ask himself is, "Do the benefits of the medicine outweigh the risks of the medicine?" There are lots of reasons to not write a prescription for an antibiotic if your patient doesn't really need it. Things like antibiotic resistance are important for the entire human population. Side effects of the medication are important for the actual patient.

One of the big side effects of antibiotics is diarrhea. Pretty much all antibiotics can cause some diarrhea, some worse than others. Patient reactions will vary greatly as well. One person could have terrible diarrhea with a specific antibiotic, and another person could have no problem at all.

As doctors we are unsure of all the reasons that antibiotics cause diarrhea. But we do know a few things, and we have some well-founded suspicions on other things.

Antibiotics kill bacteria, and our guts have a very large number of bacteria that are actually good for us and needed. We know that the antibiotics can kill these good bacteria as well as the bad bacteria that we are trying to kill. We know this can lead to poor digestion and thus to loose stools. Many theories suggest that some antibiotics are just irritating to the intestinal lining. An irritated gut can speed up movement of food and fluids through the gastrointestinal tract and lead to diarrhea.

If your child gets diarrhea from an antibiotic, it is usually going to happen after the

Istock.com/Annetka

first several days of treatment. It can some-times happen even after the course of antibi-otics is complete. Usually the diarrhea is char-acterized by loose, watery stools two to five times per day and isn't associated with a lot of pain or gassiness. Usually these loose stools aren't severe enough to warrant stopping the antibiotics. It is important that if your child ever has excessive amounts of diarrhea (more than six per day), that you let your child's doc-tor know.

Can there ever be any issues with the diar-rhea caused by antibiotics? The answer has to be yes, of course there could be. The most prevalent is a rash on the bottom from all the loose stools. This is most common in children who are still in diapers and is usually treated with some extra diaper cream. Dehydration could be a concern with excessive amounts of diarrhea, but this is very rare.

Another rare complication is an infection with Clostridium difficile. These bacteria can be present in the gastrointestinal tract with no symptoms. Your normal balance of gut bacteria stops it from becoming an issue. Antibiotics can kill the healthy bacteria that are normally keeping C diff in check. C diff then starts to become the predominant bac-teria, which can lead to a condition known as colitis. Colitis can result in foul-smelling stools that will become more frequent, possi-bly containing blood and mucus. If you sus-pect this condition, let your doctor know as soon as possible.

Usually with the diarrhea caused by anti-biotics, the treatment is just to increase fluids and make sure your child stays hydrated. Add some diaper rash cream if the baby is still in diapers to either prevent a diaper rash or treat one that is starting. If the diarrhea ever becomes excessive or painful, then let your child's doctor know right away. Also watch for mucus and blood in the stool, and alert your doctor right away if you see them.

Usually, the diarrhea will resolve once the antibiotics are finished. The healthy gut bacteria will return in time. As physicians, we may try to speed this up by adding some probiotics to the baby's diet. This is a dose of good bacteria to help replenish what the antibiotics killed. This can be done by adding yogurt to the baby's diet, or by adding dietary supplements to his food. Older children who can swallow a pill can also take it orally.

TAKE-HOME POINTS:

1. Antibiotics cause side effects, and diarrhea is probably the most common.
2. The diarrhea usually isn't bad and will go away on its own.
3. If the diarrhea ever becomes excessive, has blood or mucus in it, leads to dehydration, or your child is having a lot of abdominal pain, let your doctor know.

Why are fevers always higher at night? / Why do fevers start at night?

Millions of frustrated parents out there are painfully aware that fevers tend to either appear or spike at the *exact* hours the doctor's office is closed. Many of you have hurried your child to the ER in the wee hours because of this cruel juxtaposition of body physiology and business hours. Most of the time it ends with the ER attending physician assuring you nothing is wrong and sending you home. Well, nothing may be wrong with your child, but that ER visit has wreaked havoc on your sleep for the night and will attack your wallet in the near future. Let's talk about how to ease everyone's suffering here.

We all know that a normal body temperature is 98.6°F, right? Right??

WRONG!

You see, 98.6°F is an *average* body temperature. Our body will naturally fluctuate a degree in each direction throughout the day.

This means that a normal body temp can range from 97.6°F to 99.6°F, right doc? Sweet, I get it now. Thanks for the explana—

WRONG! Listen up!

These temperatures are the *average*. Body temps actually follow one of those bell-shaped curves, also called a normal distribution curve. About 84 percent of people fall in

Istock.com/skynesher

that curve, with 7 percent of people falling above that range and 7 percent falling below it. A child or an adult could have a body temp of 97.2°F, 96.9°F, 99.3°F, or any number of other spots along that curve and be perfectly fine. No cause for alarm whatsoever. So where is the line? I'm glad you asked. The medical community has decided that anything at or over 100.4°F is a fever. Once you have crossed that line, congratulations, you're in Feverville.

Now that we have covered what fevers are and how body temp works, let's get back to where this conversation started.

Why? Why do they only come at night? I must know!!

Part of the reason fevers come at night is due to kid behavior. During the day, even if the child has a fever, he is probably mostly doing what kids do. He is getting dirty, playing, running around, etc. like kids do. Hey, if Jordan can hang 38 on Utah while dehydrated and puking from food poisoning, your child can build a LEGO tower with a slight fever. He appears perfectly normal all day, but until you touch him you don't notice it. Sometimes, he gets into really messy stuff and touching them isn't even an option until soap and water have been properly applied. In the case of babies, he can be poopy, wet, slimy, or covered in strained peas, and thus you're more focused on cleaning him up than noticing a fever. This is all part of a normal day parenting, and it can delay detection. If the child seems fine, acts fine, and doesn't complain/cry, how would you know anything is wrong? The answer is simple—you wouldn't.

This is just part of the explanation, but not all of it. It is also true that temps tend to rise either late at night or early in the morning. The reason has to do with fluctuation of our normal body steroids. It's a bit over-complicated to discuss the what's and how's of our body's steroid system here, so just know our normal body steroids tend to dip at night between 9 p.m. and 4 to 5 a.m. This dip produces the conditions in the body that allow a fever to jump a couple ticks. So, the kid may have had a slight fever all day, and then night comes when they lay down. All is quiet. Anyone who has had a headache and tries to go to bed understands what a futile gesture that can be. When all is quiet and still, conditions like headaches and fevers are more noticeable. If the fever comes on slowly during the night, this is why a child will go to bed feeling fine and wake up with a fever. He probably went to bed with a slight rise in temp, but he felt fine and thus didn't say anything. Overnight, the fever takes advantage of the body conditions and then it's morning and, well, you know the rest.

So, see? It isn't a conspiracy. Normal kid activity coupled with some body functions and the enhanced sensitivity that comes with getting ready for bed all work together to send that mercury rising at nighttime. It's perfectly normal to notice these things at night, or first thing in the morning. It's not any less frustrating, but it's normal.

What you've learned is good information, but it doesn't really change anything. Though parents easily freak out over a high temp, doctors very rarely do. I AM NOT telling you to ignore a very high fever (and be sure to see the exceptions below regarding children under two months of age or those who have recently had surgery), but generally we are more concerned that they *have* a fever rather than how high it is. It is important that you accurately measure the child's temperature. Ask your doctor how they prefer you to take a temperature. Telling your doctor the time and temperature measured is important. After your child is older than two months of age a normal office visit the next day or so should be all that is needed. A child with a fever that truly needs to go to the ER is pretty rare. Use your own judgment of course, but if your child is running a mild fever, feels a little ill, and the doc can see you in a reasonable amount of time, skip the ER. The rest that you will both get at home, rather than hanging out in the lobby of a hospital all night will likely do you more good than visiting the ER.

IMPORTANT!! Rules always have exceptions, and this is more of a guideline than a rule. So, yes, there are exceptions. If you have a baby less than two months old that develops a fever, do not wait. See a doctor immediately. If it is outside normal office hours GO TO THE ER. A newborn less than two months old with a fever is ALWAYS an emergency. Another circumstance is if the child has had a surgical procedure recently. Contact the doctor/hospital that performed the surgery and see them right away if possible. If they are not available, GO TO THE ER. There could be a complication from the procedure, and if that's the case it needs to be addressed immediately.

So, to sum up:

1. Fevers are more likely to start and be higher during the night, or first thing in the morning.

2. A fever is any temperature above 100.4°F.
3. A fever by itself is not a reason to rush to the emergency room, unless your child is less than two months old or has had recent surgery.

When you call your doctor, you need to provide the following information to help them to help you:

1. The actual temperature taken by a real thermometer. Let them know how you took the temperature. Only give them the number the thermometer actually said.
2. Let them know of any other symptoms present. It is important to know whether your child has had any runny nose, cough, vomiting, diarrhea, etc. Keep track of how long those symptoms have been going on for.
3. It's important to tell your doctor if your child has had any exposures to illnesses in the home or at daycare. Are any of their friends / family sick? Other kids at daycare? Your doctor also needs to know of any recent foreign travel, including when and where you were.
4. It makes life easier if you also know your child's weight and any medicines he is taking. If you find yourself talking to a doctor other than your child's regular pediatrician, be sure and inform her of any ongoing medical conditions.

Why is RSV so scary in a baby?

RSV? What the heck is RSV, and why do I need to be scared? If you are like most parents starting out, you've never even heard of RSV. It won't take long to hear of it after finding out you're going to have your first baby. People will speak of it much the same as you would have expected people hundreds of years ago to have talked about the plague.

So, what is it?

RSV is the abbreviation for the Respiratory Syncytial Virus. (Now you know why it gets abbreviated.) It is a very common respiratory virus that is usually seen every winter and is characterized as mild for basically everyone except babies and very young children. For most people it will include a mild cough,

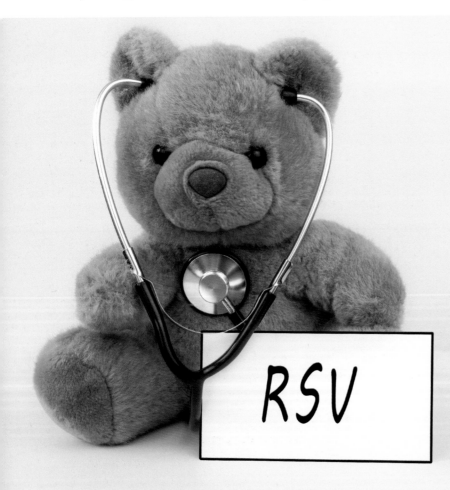

Istock.com/blueshot

runny nose, and maybe a low-grade fever the first two days. It usually lasts seven to fourteen days. For most people, it requires no treatment and goes away on its own. But, in a baby it is a completely different story.

In a baby, RSV can cause a condition known as bronchiolitis. The bronchioles are the smallest airways in your lungs right before it gets to the air sacs known as alveoli. The "itis" means inflammation. Bronchiolitis is therefore the inflammation of the bronchioles in the lung. You have heard the term "upper respiratory infection"; well, in the case of bronchiolitis it is a "lower respiratory infection." The infection in these small airways causes the lining to swell, secrete mucus, and even shed some of the cells lining the airways. All of this leads the airways to be smaller than normal and leads to wheezing and difficulty breathing.

The babies at highest risk for having problems with breathing are the smallest babies. Babies born premature with smaller airways and more immature lungs are at the highest risk. It is very common for babies less than two months of age to end up in the hospital if infected with RSV. Babies less than six months of age have a chance of hospitalization due to problems breathing or dehydration. After six months they tend to be very sick, but have less chance of ending up in the hospital. After the age of two years, RSV is usually just diagnosed as a common cold. It has a higher likelihood than the normal cold of causing a secondary ear infection.

Symptoms of RSV include: runny nose, congestion, fever, and a very deep and productive cough. Signs that your baby is having a hard time breathing with RSV would include wheezing and what we call retractions. Retractions are indentations between the ribs, under the rib cage, or above the clavicle. These indentations indicate that the baby is using the muscles in his chest wall to help him to breathe. A very rapid respiratory rate is also worrisome.

Babies that end up in the hospital might require IV fluids due to getting dehydrated from not eating or drinking, fever, and breathing faster. Some need oxygen to help with their respiratory distress. Sometimes they just need better suction of their nose and throat in order to get oxygen in through the thick and slimy snot that is in the way. If the RSV leads to secondary infections, then the baby might need some antibiotics as well.

RSV has the power to scare the parents in the "know," and rightfully so. After twenty years of practice it still has my respect, especially in very small babies. My advice to parents is, "Don't pay so much attention to how the baby sounds." If I listened to them, I'd be tempted to admit them all. Pay more attention to how the baby looks. If he looks like he is doing poorly, if he looks like he is having problems breathing, if he looks dehydrated, then take him to the hospital." If you have a very little baby, don't be brave! Always ask for help if you are feeling scared for his health.

There are some simple things you can do to significantly lower risk. Good handwashing does wonders to stop the spread of common viruses like RSV. Avoiding crowds during the peak season for RSV is also a great idea. Usually the winter months are a great time to avoid crowded stores and church with a very small baby. Remember, RSV in an adult is a very mild cold. An adult with RSV will likely think she is fine, just a case of the sniffles. Make sure everyone is washing their hands before holding your baby. Make sure if visitors work with children that they change their clothes before coming over to visit. I also try to get the school-aged sibs to change clothes as well when coming home from school.

TAKE-HOME POINTS:

1. RSV stands for Respiratory Syncytial Virus and is one of the viruses that causes the common cold, except in small babies.

2. Bronchiolitis is caused by RSV and is characterized as a very deep and wet cough, very thick mucus, wheezing, and difficulty breathing.

3. RSV in a little baby that causes problems breathing needs to be assessed by a pediatrician to determine if the baby needs to be admitted to the hospital or to tell parents what to do at home and what to look for as signs of worsening.

4. If your doctor is not available and you are concerned for your baby's health, don't delay. Take the baby to the ER.

Why do doctors not recommend a walker for a baby?

Pediatricians have been against walkers for my entire twenty-year career. They have been trying to get them banned from existence and prevent them from being sold anywhere in the United States. So, why? What is the big deal about a baby walker?

Well, it turns out they have a pretty good reason to not like them. There is a high chance of head injuries with the use of walkers. The American Academy of Pediatrics stated in the late 1990s that 1 out of 10 babies using a walker suffered a head injury. These

Istock.com/Maria Roldan Pazos

usually occurred as a baby used its walker to plummet down a stairway or the steps on the porch. They also state that studies show it may delay a baby's development. I think we can agree that head injuries and delayed development are pretty serious issues.

Let's just start off with the reasons to even have a walker. They are a break for parents. Plain and simple, walkers were invented to give a parent a break. They entertain your kiddo so you don't have to be holding or watching her all the time. Now, you could take a seat or get something else done like laundry, cleaning or maybe some dishes. Yes, free time to do chores can be a luxury when you have a very young baby. A walker gave the parents a chance to put the baby into a movable cage that they wouldn't throw a fit in. Ahhh. It's a bit frightening from that perspective, isn't it?

Just so you know, the American Academy of Pediatrics does not factor in your sanity, laundry, or need for food in their equation. You, to them, are an autonomous baby care machine that requires no maintenance. They only look at the numbers of injuries and determine that walkers are unsafe.

So, we know that walkers were made primarily for parental care. Did they serve any other purpose? Was there a benefit to the baby at all?

Parents were told through marketing that walkers were teaching babies to walk faster by building up the muscles in their legs. This made parents feel better and likely made the squiggly line on a sales graph somewhere read favorably for walker manufacturers. The baby is building important muscles! Mom and Dad get a break! The baby is happy! Only $29.95 from Blam-O!! *Call now!*

Turns out that wasn't exactly true.

(What? An advertised product not living up to the sales pitch? Stop talking crazy, doc. In related news, scientists have discovered water is wet.)

Studies have shown that babies using a walker were actually a little behind in development when it came to sitting up, crawling, and walking. As it turns out, walkers are just a really bad idea. There have been advancements in the walker design to make them safer. They are now wider to prevent them from fitting through the normal-sized household doors, and they have a braking system to help prevent them falling down stairs. They're new and improved, I tell you! And if you call right now. . . .

They are still unsafe!! They still have head injuries associated with their use. The babies using them can move faster than they could without them. Babies given the gift of speed can smash their fingers, get to hot surfaces, and break things they might not have normally been able to get to. Trust me, your little one will start rolling, crawling, and walking faster than you are ready for. A baby not given the power of wheeled momentum is a handful already. You DO NOT want to give them any additional abilities to get themselves into more trouble than they already have.

I think the pediatricians at the Academy of Pediatrics have a point on this one. Walkers just aren't safe and serve no real purpose other than making a parent's life a little easier.

Nevertheless, there are alternatives! The AAP may think of you as a needless baby care robot, but this is America, and when a parent needs a break, the marketplace will always be here to help.

There are stationary activity centers that can be used to entertain your little one and be safe at the same time. They do have their little hiccups I want you to be aware of. You will want to research the safety of all the little toys on the center for any concerns like choking or causes of pinch injuries. They don't speed up development and can cause a small delay. They have a time limit that they can be used as far as development. They become unsafe when your child gets big enough to try and climb out on their own, as they could lead to falls and then head injuries.

By far the best thing to do for development is to let your baby be on the floor and learn how to control their environment and their own muscle actions. This does require your constant attention, and that is not always possible in the real world. The important thing to remember is that load of laundry or bit of cleaning that you could do while they are entertained in a walker will never be worth their safety. It is okay to have things for your baby to do in a safe environment where you don't have to be right beside them, but walkers are not a safe environment.

TAKE-HOME POINTS:

1. Don't use walkers; it is really that simple.
2. Walkers are a common cause of injuries in babies; just don't do it!
3. If the injuries are not enough, it will delay your baby's development.
4. Have I mentioned that you shouldn't use a walker with your baby? Don't!

Why won't my doctor just call in an antibiotic for my sick baby?

Because you have a good pediatrician!

You should never go to a pediatrician so that she will do what you want them to do. You should go to a pediatrician who does what your baby NEEDS her to do. Just because you think that your baby needs an antibiotic, does not mean that your baby needs an antibiotic. That whole four years of college, four years of medical school, and three years of residency was for a reason. It was to

Istock.com/filadendron

teach your pediatrician how to tell the difference between viruses and bacteria. When to act and when to wait, and when medication should or shouldn't be given. You know, that whole "practicing medicine" thing.

Most parents have the idea that if my baby is sick, then antibiotics will make her better. Antibiotics are only used to treat bacterial infections. Most of the illnesses your child will suffer from are due to viruses, but antibiotics won't help get rid of a viral infection. Antibiotics used on a virus will just make your child suffer from the side effects and have no effect on the virus. The side effects could actually make a bad situation worse.

So, what kinds of illnesses are caused by bacteria? The most common illnesses that we will see in children include things like ear infections, sinus infections, pneumonia, skin infections, urinary tract infections, and strep throat. These types of infections, when diagnosed as being caused by a bacterial infection, are usually treated with antibiotics.

What kinds of illnesses are caused by viruses? The most common illnesses you will see in children caused by viruses include things like the common cold, the flu, RSV, croup, gastrointestinal viruses causing vomiting and diarrhea, slapped cheek syndrome, roseola, hand-foot-and-mouth disease, and chicken pox. These viral infections usually just need time. Given time, our bodies form antibodies to fight off the illness.

Then there are even some illnesses that aren't really illnesses at all. Things like seasonal allergies can make you feel terrible with runny nose, congestion, cough, and sneezing, but you haven't been infected by anything.

We even see ill symptoms with things like diabetes, hypothyroidism, cancer, and some vitamin deficiencies. These would need to be treated differently depending on the cause of the symptoms.

See that cough that you wanted an antibiotic called in for could actually be caused by a bacterium causing a sinus infection or pneumonia (in which case you would be right) or allergies, a cold, cancer, or even reflux (in which case you would be wrong). It is important to see a doctor. Your pediatrician can determine what the cause of the symptoms are, so the right therapy can be used to treat it and do so quickly.

In today's medical schools and residencies, the words "evidence-based medicine" are used frequently. This means that the doctor needs to have proof of what they are treating and why. They should be able to easily explain to you what they are treating, how they are treating it, and what you can expect during the treatment. Let me give you an example.

Amy is a two-year-old little girl who has had a cold for seven days and now has a fever of 102°F. Her cough has gotten worse over the last 24 hours and she has just been lying around and feeling terrible. Her mom brought her to the clinic today and I looked her over. I agreed that she looked terrible and it was time to act. Her lungs sounded a little "chunky" so we did an x-ray that showed a pneumonia on the right side of her lungs. I prescribed her an antibiotic called Cefdinir and told her mom that Amy needed to take it once a day for the next ten days. She needed to avoid any vitamins with iron, because it would interfere with the absorption of the antibiotic. The antibiotics could cause some diarrhea, so I advised that she try to eat some yogurt throughout the day. I want her fever gone after 72 hours on the antibiotics. If it isn't gone within that time frame, call me back. If at any time she starts to have problems breathing, starts vomiting, or looks dehydrated call me ASAP.

The above scenario is an example of evidence-based medicine. We know we have a pneumonia, because we can see it on a chest x-ray. We have prescribed an antibiotic that we know works well with this type of pneumonia. The parent knows what to expect. He or she may see diarrhea as a side effect and if the fever isn't gone in 72 hours, they know what to do. The parent also knows what I would think were signs that she was getting worse. This is what you should expect from your doctor's visit. If you are not getting something like this experience with your pediatrician, then ask for it. If he can't provide it, it might be time to find a new doctor.

Why don't pediatricians recommend teething tablets?

I can't speak for every doctor. I am proud of the level of service I provide my patients, and I know a lot of fellow pediatricians who also are passionate about what they do. I consider those like me "Good Doctors." When I say that, I mean they care deeply about their patients. It's personal and professional to them, and to myself. I know I don't like teething tablets, and the vast majority of other "Good Doctors" I know do not recommend them either.

To be honest, there is probably something else wrong with your baby if they are

Istock.com/ideabug

that miserable. Is teething uncomfortable? Yes, of course it is. Any of us whose wisdom teeth survived until adulthood can attest to it. They should not, however, be screaming like wild banshees over it. There is a chapter in this book on crying. If the child will not stop crying, something besides teething is likely afoot.

Yet there's a more important reason that I don't recommend these things. There is also, slight as it may be, a possibility of you hurting your kid with those "natural" teething tablets.

So, why do I *hate* teething tablets?

Many people don't realize the "natural" ingredient in most of those tablets is a deadly poison. Yep. Go look at the bottle, I'll wait . . . At the top of the back sticker you'll see Active Ingredients. I'm guessing belladonna is at or near the top spot. It sounds innocent, but belladonna is from a plant called Deadly Nightshade. Now if you are looking at a deadly nightshade plant, it's quite beautiful. It is also naturally occurring, as the label promises. You know what else is naturally occurring? Grizzly bears, arsenic, avalanches, and lava—all of which are found in nature. Think of belladonna like a grizzly bear. They're both natural, beautiful, best left unmolested in their natural habitat, and strictly viewed from a distance.

Extracts from the Deadly Nightshade plant were used to make poison arrows. According to legend, the Roman Emperor Augustus was betrayed and poisoned with belladonna. When you're reading a fairy tale about an evil queen or evil godmother, this is the stuff they dump in the bottle or coat the apple with before cackling wildly. Then the poor unsuspecting princess takes a bite and, well, you know.

So, what on earth compelled anyone to take one of the deadliest plants known to mankind and put it in a teething tablet?

It does have medical applications. We've all heard the expression, all things in moderation, right? Well, extracts from the plant are currently used to make the medicines atropine (used to decrease secretions, decrease pulse or blood pressure, treat an AV block of the heart, or as an antidote to mushroom or insecticide poisoning), as well as scopolamine (a medicine used to treat nausea and motion sickness but in high doses can cause hallucinations). There have been some severe side effects and possibly even deaths due to this "natural" treatment for teething and it has *never gone through FDA trials* to prove its effectiveness or safety in babies.

Everybody cuts teeth. Though people have died trying to sooth teething pain, nobody has died from actual teething. Not all aches and pains require treatment. It is perfectly okay to be grumpy because you are cutting a tooth. It will pass. Soothe your baby, hold him, rock and cuddle him. It's pretty effective and astoundingly safer.

If your baby is having severe pain, severe fever, severe diarrhea, or severe anything, it's not from teething. There's no such thing as severe teething. If anything you would label as "severe" is happening, go see a doctor. Teething is the process of the teeth elevating through the surface of the gums. This action will cause some irritation to the gum, but that is about it. Baby should be no more than a bit fussy or grumpy.

Normal teething is unlikely to cause real fever (above 100.4°F), or diarrhea (more than six loose stools per day). How about the drooling? It is like my baby has sprung a leak. Well, a four-month-old leaking spit like a busted water main is pretty normal, even if he isn't teething.

Here's the bottom line. If you have something bad enough that you need to treat the baby with a medicine, you probably aren't dealing with teething. At that juncture, what is needed is some further investigation on your part, or possibly a talk with your doctor. The circumstance literally does not exist where giving your baby a potentially deadly poison for teething is prudent.

TAKE-HOME POINTS:

1. Don't use teething tablets. I'm not flexible on this, and you shouldn't be either.
2. Teething is a natural part of life and growing up. It is actually okay to feel some discomfort at times. It prepares you for real life.
3. Never treat your child in order to soothe yourself. Often, we are giving our children medicines because their fussiness is bothering us. Your discomfort is not a reason to medicate your child.

Why is my baby drooling and putting things in her mouth?

I don't know that I get this as a question as much as I get this as a statement. "She is teething, because she is drooling and putting things in her mouth."

In actuality, there is more to the story.

Sure, there is a good chance that she is teething. I mean, symptoms of teething do include drooling and chewing on things. However, did you know drooling and chewing on things is a normal part of development even when a child is not teething?

About the time that a baby is four months old, she starts to produce more saliva. It just happens, without warning. One day, it's like your little angel has sprung a leak.

She doesn't really know what to do with the saliva, so it just kind of leaks out their mouths. Some babies are better at swallowing it than others. Some just look like they are a fountain and are in constant need of a bib or a change of clothes.

At four months of age, another developmental stage starts showing up that adds to the mystery of teething symptoms. She starts using her mouth to explore shape and texture. Therefore, she puts everything in her mouth and bites on it. This causes parents and pediatricians to worry, but for different reasons. Parents worry that their child is teething and that they need to do something to help.

Istock.com/AnaBGD

Your pediatrician is worried they are going to choke on something. It is very normal for your child to be doing this. You do need to make sure there isn't anything around your baby they can choke on. I practice the rule that if it is small enough to pass through a toilet paper roll, it is too small to be around your baby.

So, there we have it. It is completely normal at four months for your baby to drool like a Mastiff and put everything in her mouth. You are now thinking that your whole life is a lie. You knew those had to be symptoms of teething. Now, how are you going to know if your baby is teething or not?

Fear not!

This is a book that answers questions. It is what we are supposed to be doing. A baby will get her first tooth somewhere between the ages of two months and 18 months. About half of them will have a tooth by the time they are six months old. The first tooth is usually one of the bottom front teeth, but that isn't always the case, as I have seen them come through in about every order imaginable. They can also come in with all kinds of different spacing. I have seen them get four teeth in all at the same time. I have also seen them have months in between getting a new tooth.

Symptoms of teething include drooling and chewing on things, like we already discussed. Other things that you could see are flushed cheeks, tender gums, swollen gums, watery stools, fussiness, decrease in appetite, and a slight elevation of temperature.

You should not see a real fever with teething. If their temp is above 101°F, I wouldn't think that is teething. You shouldn't see real diarrhea either. If you are having over six stools per day that are loose, I would think illness rather than teething.

Parents always want to help their children with teething pain. Most babies do fine with teething, other than being a little grumpy. If your baby is extremely fussy, check with your pediatrician for the correct dose of a pain reliever. Cold things to chew on could help. My favorite teething aid is to wet the corner of a washcloth and freeze it. The cold texture on a swollen gum seems to help quite a bit. Plus, it is fairly easy to wash the cloth and reuse. When my oldest was teething I usually had five or six of these frozen washcloths in the freezer ready and waiting.

TAKE-HOME POINTS:

1. Drooling and putting things in the mouth could be a sign of teething, but often it is just a normal developmental activity.

2. First teeth come in sometime between the age of two and eighteen months. Spacing, timing, etc. are all subject to change.

3. Don't worry about it they are teething or not. If your baby is fussy, give them some love. Those teeth will come in whether you are doing anything or not.

Why is sunscreen so important for my baby?

A baby's skin is much more sensitive than that of an adult. Studies have indicated that severe sunburn as a child is much more likely to lead to skin cancer later in life than sunburns as an adult. Severe sunburns in children are also more likely to lead to complications like dehydration, heat stroke, and infection.

Baby skin is very sensitive. If you haven't figured this out by now, you will. This is the reason you need to be careful about using things with dyes and fragrances in them. It is easy for them to get diaper rashes, and they are more likely to have skin conditions like eczema. Over time, our skin gets less sensitive. More melanin shows up in our skin to protect it from sun damage. As we get damage to our skin our body sets up defenses to prevent further damage.

In the case of a baby, though, he hasn't set up his defense mechanisms to prevent damage yet. That is why sometimes their first sunburn seems to be quite severe even though it seemed like they weren't out in the sun for very long. It is also important to remember that sunburn doesn't have anything to do with the heat. Sunburn is a reaction to excessive UV exposure. That UV exposure can happen despite clouds and overcast days, in as quickly as ten to fifteen minutes. Geography is important here too. If you live in sunny Florida, you are likely more mindful of sun exposure than someone who lives in Chicago.

Istock.com/batuhan toker

Regardless of whether you live in California, Hawaii, Minnesota, Maine, Oregon, or Alaska, you must be cautious of too much sun.

I have been taught that 80 percent of the damage that leads to skin cancer happens before you are 18 years of age. So, what are the recommendations for sunscreen? For the first several months of life, we don't want the babies out in the sun at all. This is covered elsewhere in the book, but suffice to say that in the first four months or so of life, there's no safe way to have your baby in direct sunlight. After the first four months you can slowly get them a little exposure, though you still have to be very careful about sunburns, as well as overheating. They have limited ability to sweat and cool themselves off at this stage. If your baby gets too hot, dehydration or heat-stroke could occur.

At four months of age, if going outside, we recommend covering the baby's head with a hat. Long sleeves and pants are always a good idea too. Make sure the clothing has a specific SPF (it is possible for them to get sun damage through their clothing). Apply sunscreen to their skin fifteen to twenty minutes prior to going outside. It is very important to allow the sunscreen to absorb into the skin for it to work well. Sunscreen should be applied to skin and then reapplied every two hours at least when outside and more often if being exposed to water (this is even true for water-proof sunscreens). We recommend an SPF of at least 30 for your baby. Another great idea is for your baby to wear sunglasses. Make sure they have SPF factor in them as well.

If your child ever gets a sunburn, here are a couple of tips. Cool down their skin as fast as possible. Even when you remove them from sunlight, damage can still be occurring. We recommend using a good lotion and using it often. If the sunburn blisters, do not pop the blisters. This will increase the likelihood of infection. Acetaminophen is recommended for any pain. Do not use any petroleum-based products on the skin. Do not use any of the topical pain relievers on the skin. If your child looks dehydrated, is acting lethargic, runs a fever, or has skin that starts to have red streaks or pus coming from any of the blisters, see your doctor right away. If you have a baby less than six months of age with a blistering sunburn it is a good idea to see your doctor right away.

TAKE-HOME POINTS:

1. Baby's skin is much more sensitive to sunburn than older children or adults.
2. It is your job as a parent to protect your child from sunburn. At first, they can't protect themselves, then they get older and won't.
3. Most of the damage leading to skin cancer happens as a child.
4. Sunscreen early and often, shade is good, and cover if possible. If there's any sign of burn, get out of the sun and then be even more careful with the already damaged skin.

PART 5
AFTER YEAR ONE

"When my children become wild and unruly, I use a nice, safe playpen. When they're finished, I climb out."

—*Erma Bombeck*

Istock.com/Kyryl Gorlov

Why does my baby hold his breath when he is upset?

On July 5, 1997, I had literally been a doctor for a little over a month and had been in residency for only a few days. We had just completed all our paperwork and training for CPR and pediatric advanced life support and it was my first evening four-hour rotation in the Emergency Department. Since this wasn't my Emergency Medicine rotation, I would only be seeing sick kids in the sub-acute side. These were kids that were being seen after-hours but could have easily been seen by any doctor's office if it was normal office hours.

I went into the exam room to see my first patient. This was literally my first patient ever to see since I had graduated from medical school. It was a little boy about three years old who was not having a good day. I asked all the questions and found out that this little guy had been sick for two to three days with a cold, but now was crying like he was in pain and had a fever. I started feeling a little more confident. I had this, I was already sure that this little guy was going to have an ear infection and I was going to be able to fix him. I listen to his chest . . . clear. I look at his eyes . . . clear. I go to look at his ears and he gets mad, but I calmly keep going. Suddenly he gets quiet, turns blue, and passes out. At

Istock.com/arnoaltix

that moment I turned a little white myself. I had no idea what had just happened. I ran out of the room to get a supervising physician, because I was sure that somehow, I had just looked at a kid's ear and somehow killed him. The teaching physician followed me into the room, assessed the situation, and told me I was a big dummy (by the way, emergency doctors are not that nice and those were not the words he actually used). The little one woke up; I wrote him a prescription for Amoxicillin and I had learned a lot about breath-holding spells. It was quite the memorable experience for a first patient, let me tell you.

So, what do you as a parent need to know about breath-holding spells? First off, they are really common. They typically happen in kids who are six months to six years of age, but definitely hit their peak during the terrible two's. They are a reflex and not just something kids do on purpose. This usually happens in response to them getting mad or getting hurt. In a supreme act of defiance, it's like they try to refuse something as simple as breathing. If they do it once they will typically do it again. They will cry loudly, have a pause in their breathing, start turning bright red, then gray and then a little blue, and then they will either take a breath or pass out. As soon as they pass out, they will start breathing again and they will wake up in less than a minute and be none the worse for wear. I cannot promise the same for the parents, who may be scarred for life. When you know that you have a breath-holder, you will soon learn what their triggers are and be able to avoid them.

If you have a child that has a breath-holding spell, you want to make sure he doesn't fall and hurt himself if he were to pass out. You also want to make sure he didn't pass out because he choked, so make sure and check in his mouth and make sure he starts breathing as soon as he passes out. If your child does not wake up in a minute, I would recommend calling 911. The very first time your child decides to have one of these breath-holding spells and passes out, I would also recommend you see the doctor to make sure everything is okay. After that, you will become an expert on breath-holding spells and it won't freak you out nearly as much.

The first time you deal with one, don't be too hard on yourself if you freak out a little. Just remember that freshly minted doctor who freaked out the first time he saw one happen.

TAKE-HOME POINTS:

1. Breath-holding spells are pretty common.
2. Although they are scary to watch, they usually don't hurt your child.
3. The first time your child has a breath-holding spell, get him checked out by their doctor.
4. If your child doesn't wake up in one minute, call 911.
5. If you know your child has breath-holding spells, try to avoid their triggers and if they are going to pass out try and keep them safe from falls or injury.

Why does my baby wake up screaming every night?

The story usually goes something like this:

We were fast asleep when suddenly, the baby started screaming like something had grabbed her and dragged her off into the woods. After the initial shock, we jumped out of bed to go see what was wrong. She was standing up in the bed and screaming like we had never heard her scream before. We

Istock.com/M-image

went to pick her up to calm her down and she got even worse. Her eyes were open and she was looking around, but she was fighting us like she didn't know us and even worse like we were what she was scared of. Finally, she stopped, looked around, snuggled up, and went to sleep like nothing had ever happened. The next morning, she acted like nothing ever happened.

So, what did happen?

This is a textbook example of a night terror. Night terrors usually happen in small children from the ages of six months to six years of age. They are a sleep disturbance that happens at a very specific stage of sleep. Often they will happen at the same time every night, sometimes multiple times per night and for days or even weeks in a row. They will then stop and you will go back to sleeping like normal people only to have them suddenly start back up again. Think of it as nature's way of checking on the status of your heart health.

These are often the first stage of sleep disturbances that children can develop. It is not uncommon for them to develop sleepwalking later on and then become older children or even adults who talk in their sleep. It is not unusual for them to have a parent that may have had night terrors, sleepwalking, or sleep talking in their past or may even still do it occasionally.

The basic cause of this family of sleep disturbances is a short circuit. They are happening at a time when we are supposed to have an active brain, but an inactive body. The best way I can describe it is that our brain is supposed to be dreaming and having a grand old time and our body is supposed to be turned off so it can't move or do what we are dreaming about. In these cases, the body "off" switch gets turned "on" and we start actually doing what we are dreaming about.

In the above scenario, the little girl is having a dream. She appears to be awake, standing up, screaming, and her eyes are wide open. She is not actually seeing what is really in front of her; she is seeing what is in her dream. The reason she screamed louder when she was picked up is because whatever she is dreaming about and scared by has just grabbed her. She is now even more terrified, not by you but by the "boogeyman" who just grabbed her.

We never get to know what she is scared or dreaming about. The reason for this is the difference between night terrors and nightmares. A nightmare may wake you up. You will be scared, shaking, and have an elevated heart rate and breathing fast, but you remember what you were dreaming about and why you were scared. In the case of a night terror, she has no idea it even happened. When she wakes up, she is calm and ready to go back to sleep. She will have no recollection of what she was scared of, or that it even happened.

When you figure out your child is having night terrors, you need to wake her up and calm her down. She is usually pretty easy to get back to sleep depending on how hard you had to try to get her to wake up. As soon as she really wakes up, she will usually calm down and go back to sleep.

Night terrors can just happen, but often they will have a trigger of a change in sleep. I will often find that the family has just been on vacation and changed their normal routine, or the time has changed, or the child has been sick or not sleeping normally the last several nights. Often just getting her back into her normal routine will get the terrors to stop. If nothing has triggered them, I often have parents try to mess with their sleep cycle by keeping them up a couple of nights in a row about two hours past their normal bedtime. Sometimes the very thing that can trigger night terrors can get them to stop.

TAKE-HOME POINTS:

1. Night terrors usually happen between the ages of six months and six years.
2. The difference between night terrors and nightmares is that in night terrors, the child will not remember them.
3. You will need to wake up the child to get her to stop.
4. Try to get them back into their normal sleep routine if you have recently had a change, or mess with their normal routine for two days if there haven't been any changes.

Why is my toddler refusing to poop?

Have I mentioned that becoming a pediatrician will make you an expert in poop? Yes. Yes, I have. What's that? You say you thought we were done with poop? Oh nooo . . . *never*. There's always more poop.

The common scenario goes something like this:

My baby had a stool that was a little hard and she had to push really hard to get it out. She cried a little when it came out, but she seemed okay afterward. Now she is trying not to poop! It has been a day or two since her last stool and I can tell she needs to poop. My baby just cries and cries and holds her legs together and clinches like she is trying not to poop. Please doc, tell me. What is going on here? Why doesn't my baby want to poop?

I have this conversation at least a couple of times per week. This seems to start around the age that a baby could start potty training, usually around fifteen to twenty-four months. The ability to delay waste elimination will develop on its own, whether you encourage her to use it or not.

Oh, I hear the outrage already, that a baby that young is not ready to potty train. I have heard that is too young, that it could damage their psyche, and other mindless drivel. I humbly submit this is all a bunch of crap that the diaper companies are more than happy for you to believe. The age where a baby could start potty training and the age that parents actually start doing it are often not the same for this reason.

Before the time of the disposable diaper, the average age that a baby was potty trained was around eighteen months. After the diaper companies came out with the ease of disposable diapers, it went to two years of age. When they came out with the potty-training aid of pull-ups, it delayed potty training even longer.

One of the biggest things needed in potty training is the ability to hold in urine or stool until you are in the right spot to deposit it in the potty. Again, that ability to hold it comes whether you are potty training or not. If a child has something that happens to make them afraid to stool such as a constipated stool that hurts, she will try and hold her stool and keep it from coming out. She is just a baby, and decision-making is new to her. She will make bad decisions from time to time.

Unfortunately, our colon (large intestine) is not very smart. It only knows how to absorb water. The longer the stool stays in the colon, the more water it absorbs and then guess what? Bingo! Stool gets harder and when your little bundle finally poops again it hurts even more. Now what is she going to do? She is going to try even harder to not poop. It does not take long for this cycle to spiral into being a full-blown problem.

Constipation is the enemy of potty training. It doesn't matter why the constipation is happening. If your little one starts to associate stooling with pain, it can set up a psychological vicious cycle of trying not to stool. It is

Istock.com/Juanmonino

time to call in the poop expert. Go and talk to your doctor right away. We are poo-certified to handle all sorts of poo problems.

You will find all kinds of advice online and from your friends and family. Don't take it as gospel! Go to your doctor and have a detailed plan of what to do if your child gets constipated and it hurts again. Have a plan to keep the stools soft so they don't hurt. Finally, make a plan to start potty training. If she can hold her stool to get more constipated, she can hold it and put it in her potty.

If you have a toddler that is trying not to poop and you can tell she is taking any kind of action to prevent poop from coming out, please talk to your pediatrician. This is a much bigger deal than it seems. Parents don't realize that such a small thing could affect their child for years. These issues can lead to chronic constipation, delayed potty training, and even a condition known as encopresis, where children just chronically leak stool out into their underwear all day long.

TAKE-HOME POINTS:

1. A child holding her stool is a problem that needs to be taken care of and it is best to consult your child's doctor right away.

2. Something has caused your baby to be like this. The most common problem is constipation, but even trying to prevent the feeling of stool against their skin could lead to this problem.

3. Make sure that when you go to the doctor that you leave with a plan. A plan that includes how to correct the hard stool, keep stools soft, keep stools regular, and when and how to potty train.

4. Trust your pediatrician. We are poo experts. Shy away from folk wisdom and crystals. Crystals are pretty, but they are not medicine. They are also choking hazards for your little one.

Why is my toddler refusing to eat?

I'll give you a clue. It's not because your meat loaf is dry and flavorless. It's because your toddler's appetite is a bit unpredictable. You may have already figured out it really doesn't matter who is cooking or how good it tastes. If you have arrived at that realization, good for you! You have taken the first step toward not panicking. There are 97 ½ steps remaining. Buckle up.

There are just times that your little one is going to refuse to eat. It is going to bother you, it will bother your mother, and it will bother your grandmother. Unfortunately, raising children and having the wisdom of

Istock.com/iladendron

experience is no match for this act of toddler defiance. There will be lengthy conversations on the phone and in person. Many a hand will be wringed in mental agony. Ironically, you will probably miss a meal or two of your own. You will lose sleep over this topic.

Do you know who isn't worried about this problem?

Your child. He is blissfully unaware that you are concerned about his apparent lack of calories and his impending death from starvation. He seems oblivious to the fact that his lack of eating will lead to him becoming skin and bones and just evaporating from existence. As he giggles through his journey toward emaciation, an odd thing is happening. He seems to be just as active and just as happy as ever. All seems well despite his starvation diet. Yep. He seems emboldened by his choice to refuse all sustenance, and in fact he has some energy to burn. It's absolutely maddening.

Do you know who else isn't worried about this problem?

Your pediatrician. Trust me, I have this conversation on a daily basis with very concerned and stressed parents, who are talking right beside an active, happy, and healthy child. The reason we aren't worried is because this is normal, and in a strange way, completely healthy. My running joke with parents is that I have never lost a toddler due to starvation, but I've come close to losing a couple of parents from worrying themselves to death.

A normal one-year-old is a human garbage disposal. He will eat almost everything (some of it not even food). Parents get used to this eating pattern and then somewhere between fifteen and eighteen months when it changes, they get worried. It is all part of normal growth and development. Around fifteen to eighteen months of age, a baby changes the way that it grows. Instead of a constant rate of growth, he begins to grow in spurts. Since he doesn't have a steady rate of growth, he also doesn't have a steady need for calories to sustain that growth. His appetite will soon start to follow his growth spurts. He will have times he will out-eat his parents and there will be times he eats like a bird. Both are normal.

So, what are we as parents supposed to do? It is not your job to make your child eat a certain amount. It is your job to offer him a good variety of food. When he needs it, he will eat. I strongly encourage parents not to turn food into a punishment or a reward. Those lessons will haunt them the rest of their life. Food is simply a need; turning it into a reward has dangerous consequences.

Food is the fuel that runs the engine of their body. There will be times that kids get very good gas mileage and times that they are burning through fuel like a rocket on its way to Mars. *Leave them in charge of the fueling.* Trust me, they will very rarely run out of gas.

Another thing that I strongly encourage parents not to do is this: Johnny hasn't had anything to eat all day and has refused to eat anything. Johnny will never refuse chocolate cake. I'm going to give him a piece of chocolate cake just so he has something in his stomach.

Okay, so Johnny didn't want any food, so you gave him something he really likes to entice him to eat. That's good, right? I mean I know it's cake loaded with sugar and fat, but he's a toddler and will burn those calories right off, right?

Wrong.

Johnny didn't eat anything because he didn't need anything. He is regulating his calorie intake in a very natural and healthy way. Now in this example you tempted him with something he basically can't say no to. So, he eats *when he doesn't need to* and piles on a bunch of fat and sugar calories that are useless. Those useless, empty calories are mostly stored as fat.

It is this type of mentality that can lead to obesity in childhood. You are training your child that it is okay to eat something when he has no need for it, and in fact isn't even hungry. If he hasn't eaten anything today and you have been offering it, it is incredibly likely that everything is fine. Is your child acting normal, with normal levels of energy and such? If the answer is yes, then there's no need to worry about it.

TAKE-HOME POINTS:

1. Your child will, at some point, most likely go on what appears to be a hunger strike.
2. Your child will have different caloric needs at different points in their life.
3. Offer your child a good variety of foods and he will eat when he needs to.
4. Don't tempt your child when he doesn't need to eat.
5. Don't offer him unhealthy choices to stimulate his appetite.
6. Try not to turn food into a reward or a punishment.

Why is my toddler throwing temper tantrums?

I put toddler in the title because it is hard to define an age, but this is going to apply to your fifteen-month-old as well as to your four-year-old. Our basic problem is a failure to communicate. Well, I guess a failure to communicate maturely. Because let me assure you, toddler meltdowns communicate a distinct message very clearly.

Let me explain.

Around fifteen months or so, kiddos start to become more independent. They're starting to walk, feed, and even dress themselves.

Istock.com/Juanmonino

These great things for them to learn come with a feeling of independence. Now they want to do all these things when they want to and how they want to. Perhaps it is because they learned how to do it recently and are particularly proud of their methods.

What I wouldn't give to hear their internal dialogue. *Mom, you said put the pants on. You didn't say not on my head. They're ON. What's the problem?*

When they don't get their way, they throw a fit. Fits can range from mild frustration to a full-blown explosion. Most parents have at least one story of the time their toddler melted down in an epic fashion. I have seen it all. I have seen a toddler fit be simply crossing their arms with a loud HMMPH! I have seen bits of two-year-old shrapnel flying in all directions like someone opened a clown car at a wrestling match. Rattles flying, fists pounding the earth, and tears. Oh, the tears can get real.

A toddler is the most selfish person on the planet. In his world, everyone is here to make him happy. It's like a social media influencer, only worse. You can just unfollow an Instagram feed. There is no simple mouse click to get out of this one, however. Every need and want should be provided to him as he wants it, when he wants it. If that doesn't happen, then the train tends to come off the tracks. Then comes the meltdown, again ranging somewhere between mild discomfort and Chernobyl.

Remember, temper tantrums will look different from child to child. The one I mentioned earlier with the crossed arms and the HHMMPH! is honestly just kind of cute. I

can't help it; something about asserting their defiance with some level of sophistication is adorable.

In the not-so-adorable department, some toddlers will just scream. Not crying, mind you, at least not exclusively crying. I am constantly amazed how so much sound can come from such a tiny human. Just to keep parents guessing, another method is crying and attempting to look pitiful. They may even go silent. You may see them throw themselves down and beat the ground with their hands and feet. They may bang their heads against the floor or the wall. Some may even resort to violence and hit someone, bite someone, or throw things with the intent to break something or hurt someone.

In truth, tantrums have many forms. They have the same root cause, and here's what you can do to control them.

Your child feels the issue is communication. He feels very strongly that if you could understand the how and the why he does not want to sit in the high chair, things would be better. In fact, he thinks his way is far superior to your way and you should let him make the decisions around here. He is developing the skills to live in the world, and he is exceedingly proud of his first draft.

This is why tantrums tend to disappear after a child is four years old or so. As his communication and life skills grow, he understands why taking the fish out of the aquarium for some fresh air is a bad idea. Be sure and enjoy the time between five and thirteen years, because when children are thirteen, they lose their mind and ability to understand all over again. The fits return, but at least they don't tend to flop on the floor and rage against the linoleum anymore. Teenage fits are more like enhanced whining.

The important thing for you as a parent to understand is that a temper tantrum is your child's way to punish you. Unfortunately, it is *very* effective. You need to learn a little reverse psychology to combat temper tantrums. The child is rewarded if you give in, and he wins if you get mad. He is growing and asserting. This is normal. You have to assert who is in charge, and you can do it while allowing his psyche to continue to grow.

Think about when you punish him. If he never does the bad thing again, the punishment worked. If he cries and is sad, the punishment worked. If he is happy and goes right back to doing it again, you will not be trying that particular punishment again. Children pick up on this methodology.

So, do your best to ignore a temper tantrum. Remember, he isn't really in absolute despair. This is for your benefit. Walk away and ignore him. Try to never give in to his demands and try not to act annoyed. Act like he is not even there. Eventually, he will try and find something else with which to punish you, but none will be as effective as the temper tantrum. By not being affected, you take away his secret weapon. If his tantrum doesn't work on you, he will stop doing it.

Remember that "no" is a very confrontational word and best avoided. That word takes the control from the child. Since he "knows" that the world revolves around him, you are threatening that. When you try to take absolute control, there will be an epic smackdown.

Avoid setting yourself up for the "no." This is parental chess; you need to be thinking three moves ahead. Have alternatives, distract the child, and try to avoid the situation. Trust me, there are ways to avoid the simple "no" and the temper tantrum that follows. It doesn't mean that you spoiled him. Remember, he still didn't get whatever it was that he wanted. All you did was refuse to be punished. You didn't cause any harm. He is learning that temper tantrums are not useful forms of communication, and that's a good thing. Plus, it helps prevent him from going Defcon 1 in the cereal aisle, which can lead to a trip to the wine aisle.

TAKE-HOME POINTS:

1. Temper tantrums are a normal stage of development.
2. When you know the root cause of a meltdown, it makes it easier to avoid them.
3. Remember, when your child is getting mad, chances are he thinks you don't understand him and he is frustrated.
4. Temper tantrums will eventually end when the child learns to communicate better and develops the ability to rationalize.
5. Try to avoid "no," and your life will be much easier.

Why is my toddler biting?

If there was ever a topic that caused parents more distress than this one, I don't know what it is. My first child was the bitee. He came home from daycare two to three times with a note that he had been bitten. I remember looking at the teeth marks on his arm and thinking I wanted to go to daycare and make dental impressions of all those children and find the culprit who had hurt my baby. I curbed my desire to go all CSI Daycare, and since then I have had to deal with parents on the other side. Their baby is the biter and being threatened with being kicked out of daycare. They are worried and want to make it stop, too. They also are concerned about other kids being hurt. I have had several who have been kicked out, and it is disheartening. So, what is happening here? What can be done to stop it?

Biting is actually very common and extremely predictable. It is usually going to happen between the ages of fifteen months and two and a half years of age. Most of the time, the biting child will be cutting molars. The biting child will usually fall into one of three categories. The two most common are they are the newest member of the class or the oldest member of the class. The newest kid just needs to get things started off right and let everyone know she is not to be messed with. The oldest member is just showing that new little whippersnapper who the boss is. The last little biter falls into the group that has been bitten before or picked on. He is just repeating what he has learned, or looking for any avenue to defend himself from the pack.

Now, the first time a little one bites it may come as a complete surprise, but after that he

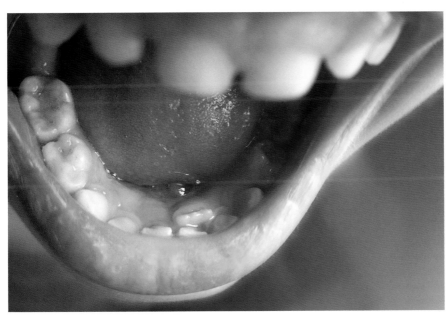

Istock.com/Tatyana Kolchugina

is predictable. He is going to bite when provoked. It will happen when someone tries to back him into a corner, take his toy, or get in his space. He has the look of a hungry wolverine right before it pulls out the fangs and goes for blood. Although daycare likes to shift the blame to the child, the fault is on the daycare worker. If those at the daycare were looking for the signs, they could intervene and prevent the trauma. It is a developmentally normal defensive maneuver that has been going on as long as there have been toddlers with teeth.

So, what are you as a parent to do if you have a child who is biting? Learn the triggers your child has that are leading to the biting and share them with everyone so they can keep them from being triggered. Know that you will need to watch this child a little closer to prevent them from biting someone. Watch them and you will also see what they look like and do right before they bare their fangs, and that will go a long way toward preventing bites from happening.

Know that it will end eventually. Chances are the child will convert to something like hitting someone upside the head with toys (arguably worse), but hey, the biting will stop. When it stops, rejoice. You have to savor the little victories.

When will it stop? I usually see it stop around the time the child gets all his molars in and he will start learning to talk. After he learns to talk, it gives him a way to express his thoughts, fears, and displeasures.

What can you do if your child is a biter and getting threatened to be kicked out of daycare? Talk to the daycare, tell them that this is a developmentally normal behavior and just like any other normal behavior that we would like to suppress, they will need to work with you to make it happen. Share with them the triggers you found and any signs that you see before your child goes to bite. Let them do the same with you. Showing that you acknowledge the problem and are working with them goes a long way. Just remember they are dealing with an angry set of parents on the other side whose little angel has your child's teeth marks embedded in their skin.

TAKE-HOME POINTS:

1. It is a normal developmental behavior for children to bite.
2. It is normally seen between the ages of fifteen and thirty months of age.
3. It is more common in the newest in the class, the oldest in the class, or a child who has been bitten before.
4. There will be triggers that set off a biter and clues that he is going to bite . . . know them both.
5. If you have a biter, make sure you talk to the daycare and let them know you will work with them, share information, and make a plan together.

Why is my child having growing pains?

It's a great question, and it's also a question that 20 to 40 percent of parents are going to ask, since it happens that often in children. So, let's dive in and see if we can clear some stuff up.

First off, growing pains often get called "bone pain," and this is wrong. It would be best described as muscle pain. We do see "growing pains" happen during the periods when children experience very rapid phases of growth, but the pain is not from their bones hurting as they grow. We see growing pains occur during the ages of two to six years old and then again from about nine to twelve years of age. They will usually occur more at night and your child could wake up crying in pain if they are bad.

What causes them? We think there are two different causes to this pain. The first cause is damage. Kids are not very nice to

Istock.com/dragana991

their bodies. They are always jumping, running, falling, and running into things. Then they have to heal, which can hurt sometimes. The second cause is growing; bones grow faster than muscles and tendons, and when they are having rapid phases of growth the muscles and tendons have to be stretched to catch up. That stretching can cause pain.

So how do we know it's growing pains and not something much worse? Everyone has heard the horror story of a parent that was told by their doctor their child had growing pains and it ended up being a bone tumor, so how do we know?

To start off, if it were growing pains, we would have a history of a child complaining of multiple different sites hurting—not at the same time, but that she may have complained of the right leg this week and last week it was the left leg. The child should like you to rub the area that hurts when she is having growing pains, but the bad things will hurt worse when they are touched or rubbed.

The other potential causes of such pain that we as doctors are going to be trying to rule out are bone tumors, cancer, arthritis, and infections of bone or joints. How do we do it? Mostly by the anecdotal evidence and by an exam. We always worry if the story is about just one joint or just one spot. If you say that you saw any swelling or redness or felt warmth you will get our attention. If we see anything while we are doing an exam, it will set off an alarm.

If anything looks or sounds different, what will a doctor order to work up the bad things? We as doctors can usually make ourselves feel a lot better with a couple of simple blood tests and maybe an x-ray. If these look normal, we will usually calm you and ourselves down. If abnormal, then more bloodwork or studies could be ordered.

If your child is having pain that you are thinking might be growing pains, just talk to your doctor, rub the painful area if they want you to, and use some ibuprofen or a heating pad on the area. They tend to last a week or so, and more often at night. They will go away only to show up again on some night when you are deep asleep and probably having the best dream of your life.

TAKE-HOME POINTS:

1. At some point, your child might have growing pains.
2. These can happen with young, active children and older children as well.
3. If you don't see or feel anything, a good rub, some pain relievers, and attention will usually take care of the problem.
4. If you see redness, feel warmth, or see any swelling, it is time to go see the doctor.

Why does my child's foot turn in when walking?

I could have titled this "Why does my child's foot turn in? Why does my child's foot turn out? Why are they bowlegged? Why is my child now knock-kneed?", but that seems a little excessive. This little section is to answer the most common questions that come up with your toddler and how they walk. Trust me, this is probably going to answer a lot of the questions your family will ask you and save you some worry.

We are going to start off with your child being bowlegged, medically known as genu

Istock.com/Sasiistock

varum. The reason we start there is because your baby starts there, too. There is an old wives' tale that states that if you stand your baby up too much on their legs you will make them bowlegged. I have a love/hate relationship with this particular type of old wives' tale. The reason I love it is because it is always correct. The reason I hate it, is the two things have nothing to do with each other. Most babies are bowlegged. They just are made that way. It will correct as they stand on them and learn to walk. Isn't it funny that the old wives' tale actually got it backwards? Them standing too much or too early doesn't cause them to have bowed legs. Conversely, it is what will eventually correct the bowed legs.

The medical term for bowed legs is tibial torsion. Most of the bowing of the legs happen from the knee down. This occurs because of the positioning of the legs while mom is pregnant. As they learn to stand and walk, the normal pressures will cause bone remodeling and repositioning. The condition will usually correct itself by the time they are two to three years old. If your child is still bowlegged after age three, it is probably time to discuss this with your pediatrician.

Now, before we discount bowed legs as being nothing to worry about, there are a few medical conditions that can lead to bowed legs. Things like rickets from vitamin D deficiency, Blount's disease caused by abnormal growth of the upper part of the tibia, or a difference in the length of the two legs. Your doctor should be evaluating your baby's legs at each well-child visit for the first two years of life—just one of the reasons they take off all of their clothes for a well visit.

Next on the list is knock-knee, or genu valgum. This is what naturally happens next in your baby. She will go from there being too far of a space between her knees to her knees angling in and touching. This is the normal alignment between the ages of two to five years of age. If it is going to happen, it should show up by the time she is four years of age. A genu valgus alignment showing up after the age of six is a reason to talk to your doctor.

There are things we have to worry about that can cause a child to be knock-kneed. It can be caused by rickets, osteomalacia, trauma to the leg bone, or even seen in severe cases of obesity in adolescents and adults. Rickets needs to be diagnosed and treated. Osteomalacia can usually be cured with vitamin D and a calcium supplement. Obesity needs to be addressed for many reasons other than just the fact that your child is knock-kneed, but this alignment problem can lead to long-term joint problems.

The next thing on the list is turning the foot in or out. We are going to talk about both of these at the same time, because they happen at the same time and usually for very similar reasons.

Turning the foot in is called pigeon toes or intoeing. This is very common in children and they usually outgrow it. It can be caused by three things.

- Tibial torsion (the same thing that led to your baby being bowlegged).
- Femoral anteversion, which is an inward twist of the thigh bone. All babies have some of this and it corrects with time.

- Metatarsus adductus (a curving of the actual foot), which is commonly caused by positioning in the uterus. Sometimes it is an actual club foot that needs treatment with casting and surgery.

Most of the causes of intoeing will correct themselves during the same time period that bowlegged will start to disappear. If it is severe or fails to correct on its own, then it is something to address with your pediatrician.

Out-toeing or turning the foot out is also common, but less common than intoeing. It happens at the same time as intoeing and is caused by flat feet, external rotation of the hip from in-utero positioning, or external tibial torsion. It does run in families and usually has no problems associated with it. Some children or adults will start to have a limp or pain at the hip, thigh, knee, or foot. Treatment is often symptomatic or with the use of orthotic inserts in the shoes. Most of the children will outgrow this condition with time.

TAKE-HOME POINTS:

1. Your baby will be bowlegged, and you did not cause it by them standing too early.
2. Your baby will probably have knock-knee as he grows up from two to five years of age.
3. There is a good chance your baby will turn his feet in or out while learning to walk. If it causes any problems or pain let your doctor know, but he will usually outgrow these as well.
4. Anytime you have any concerns you should always talk to your pediatrician, but most of the time all these conditions will resolve on their own.

Why does discipline need to start as a baby?

Discipline is a tough subject with a lot of parental interest. There have been countless books written and purchased about the subject. There is an opinion from every parent, grandparent, and casual observer that you meet, and each will offer a different view. Many of these views will be shared with you against your will. Everything you read and hear will only leave you feeling more confused. If you took the top three books on the subject, at any given time, they probably contradict each other in significant ways.

Istock.com/nanausop

Think about that for a minute. If there were three books on changing the oil in your car, Thai cooking, or gardening, they would likely agree with each other for the most part. It's not like one Thai cookbook would go rogue and claim you shouldn't use coconut milk *ever*, or the gardening book would claim azaleas are a salad vegetable. On the subject of discipline, however . . .

So, what are you left to do? You could resign yourself to trying to incorporate all the different methods everyone forcefully shares with you. That would likely lead to you driving yourself completely bonkers in a very short time frame. So, what's the plan then?

Well, in my experience as a parent and as a pediatrician, kids are unique and discipline is not a one-size-fits-all approach.

Discipline is all about consistency, which starts from the moment your child is born. Too many times parents equate discipline with punishment, but discipline is actually the combination of rewards and punishment to get to a desired goal. I humbly submit that rewards are many times more effective than punishments. These positive reinforcements should start as soon as you begin talking, laughing, and playing with your baby. Also remember that that first frowny face you gave her when she was bad was a punishment. From the very beginning, be consistent.

What's most important when it comes to discipline is that you know your own child. No one will be able to tell you how to discipline your child better than you because no one will know her as well as you do. Know what makes your child happy, makes her sad, and makes her angry. Pay attention to the things she likes to do and play with the most. What activities does she place the most importance on in her life? These things will tell you how to discipline your child when she has acted inappropriately. As an example, my oldest child was very eager to please and wanted to make me happy all the time. A simple snap of my fingers would make him cry and was punishment to him. My youngest child, if you were to snap your fingers at him, he would be more likely to dance than to cry. Thus, the discipline had to be different.

You will need to have more than one approach. You need strategies that vary in severity, and you need disciplinary approaches that you can use in different environments. You will have to be constantly revamping your strategies as your child grows.

Never hit your child or intentionally hurt them. Pediatricians have been working for years to stop the parenting style that uses spanking, hitting, slapping, or biting. This will only teach children to respond with violence when angry. When angry, people tend to be more aggressive and hit harder than they realize. Most parents accused of child abuse never meant to hurt their child, but lost control when angry. If hitting or hurting your child isn't something you do, then you don't have to worry about being too aggressive when angry.

TAKE-HOME POINTS:

1. Disciplinary action needs to be instantaneous for a small child. Young children do not have a very long memory. But they need to remember what they did and that the punishment is attached to that specific bad behavior. This is not as important in older children, as the dreaded wait for the punishment to happen is sometimes punishment itself.

2. Discipline needs to be consistent. Everybody that is going to be in an authoritative position needs to know the punishments and administer them in the same way. A soft parent or grandparent can quickly submarine good parenting efforts.

3. As much as possible when you are disciplining your child, you need to be calm. If you can't be calm, you may need to wait until you can do so. Remember that sometimes children receive positive reinforcement by making you mad (i.e., they punished you by making you mad and they are happy about it). Trying to remain as calm as possible also goes a long way in making sure you don't hurt your child.

4. Always remember that you are big and they are small. Parents choose lots of disciplinary tactics. You have no idea how hard you are grabbing them, pulling them or spanking them because you are big, sometimes ten times as big. How big a deal is that size difference? Drop a one-pound weight on your toe and then a ten-pound weight and then let's talk. (Please don't actually drop a big weight on your toe. It will hurt. A lot.)

5. Create a sliding scale of disciplinary strategies and a predetermined ranking of crimes. Kids don't always deserve a life sentence. Some things need a slight nudge, where others need a complete change of direction. For example, in our house the ranking of the crime goes way up if you deliberately hurt another child or sibling or if you are deliberately dishonest.

6. Be on the same page as your co-parent. You need to have the same rules, or this is never going to work. This may require some compromise on both your parts to find a middle ground that is acceptable to both.

7. Remember that just because it worked today doesn't mean it will work tomorrow. Your child is constantly changing and learning. The opposite is true as well, in that what didn't work today may be a great approach at another time.

So, remember my best advice about discipline: you are the only one that knows your child well enough to figure out which form of discipline will work with your precious and unique child.

Why did I write this book?

One of the coolest things about medical school was learning the "Why's." There were so many of them. I remember thinking it was so cool learning about "Old Wives' Tales" and how they came into being and where the truth stopped and the fantasy began. As I got into pediatric practice, I quickly found out that parents had a laundry list full of why's and it wasn't just fascination for them, it was often terror. I've spent the last twenty years listening to parents and gathering up the different "Why" questions that they ask in order to assemble this book.

That still doesn't answer the question, why did I want to write this book?

First, I really like to help people. Medicine is a noble calling, and I think most who do it truly want to help people. I am no different. I love to help people and always have. In my practice, I help parents through these questions on a daily basis. By writing this book I can help parents who I will never have the chance to meet. I can answer the questions they have that they won't always remember to ask their own pediatrician. I have found that parents worry a lot. We know in medicine that

Istock.com/pablohart

stress and worry are not good for your health. I also know that doctor's appointments come with a delay. Wouldn't it be nice to have a book you could go to and get your answer right away without having to wait until your baby's doctor appointment rolls around? My hope is that by answering these questions, parents will calm down, have less stress, and enjoy their children more.

Second, I wanted to leave a legacy. I want to leave the practice of pediatrics better than when I joined. In order to do that, I need to contribute something that will outlast me. By no means am I arrogant enough to think that this book will become a classic of parenting literature and will last throughout eternity. I do think that the answers in this book will help some of the parents who read it, and they will be better parents because of it. That, in a small way, passes some of my knowledge to the next generation and even the next after that. Wouldn't it be great if all of us strove to make the world a little better because we were here?

Third, I love trivia. I love the little why's of life. This book has allowed me to dive deeper into the reason that different things happen. I have been told many times that as a physician we need to always be learning. I have found that you never learn as much as you do when you teach something. In an odd way, writing this book will make me a better doctor for my patients. Even if my patients never read this book, they will get to benefit from the thought I had to put into writing this book and I will pass down the knowledge in person.

Finally, there is this little subject of competition. My oldest son decided to write a book when he was in the first grade. He went on to write a book in second grade and another in third. He is very proud of the fact that he has written two more books than I have and that he has sold more copies than I have. I can't let that just lie. Even though I am much older than him, I have to give him some competition by trying to write at least as many books as him and hopefully beat him in the copies sold department.

I really hope that you find this book helpful and it answers the most common questions you will have that revolve around the word "Why." Of course, there is a never-ending list of questions that we as parents have during our tenure as a parent. I have no way or desire to try and answer them all. I hope that we have managed to cover the most common questions that most parents come up with. I in no way am trying to replace your pediatrician with this book, and thank goodness they are there so they can help you with all the questions you will ask that didn't make the book.

Trust me, in spite of all the inadequacies we as parents feel whenever we are confronted with a question of "Why" and we don't know the answer, parenting is the most satisfying job you will ever have. It will also be the hardest and most likely the longest job you will ever have. I wish you the best in your parenting journey. My sincerest hope is that you never ask the question, "Why did I waste my time and money on this book?"

I hope you don't just survive parenting; I hope you THRIVE!

Cliff James

Lizzy Love Photography

Cliff James lives in Oak Ridge, Tennessee, with his wife Kristi, sons Dalton, Tyler, and Kaden, as well as some critters. He works in a busy pediatric practice and has the time of his life doing what he knows he was meant to do—take care of children. He is the founding physician of Kids Central Pediatrics and the author of the book *A First Time Parent's Survival Guide: A How-To-Manual for the First Two Years*.

My story started September 30, 1969. I remember it being a warm, sleepy experience when I was suddenly awoken to bright lights, loud noises, and someone smacking me on my bootie. It was then I realized I was naked as a jaybird and have had a fear of public nudity ever since. Some guy with one foot in the grave was holding me by one foot, and I saw a smiling tired lady with long, dark hair and a dude with a silly smile. The old guy asked what my name should be. Obviously not in his most creative mood, the dude with the silly smile just gave his name and slapped another number at the end of the name.

I grew up in the middle of nowhere surrounded by children, because the tired lady and guy with the silly smile thought they should have a lot of kids. My dad was aiming for four sons. When it was all said and done he was blessed with one son and four daughters. My dad, the guy with the silly smile, was a hard worker, mom was making home (her job had some kind of title like that), and we five kids were busy making lots of messes and a bunch of noise.

My grandma told me that I was going to grow up and become a pediatrician and it seemed like a good idea. I attended West Texas State University and obtained a degree in Biology. With this degree you were given the choice of starving to death or continuing your education, so I elected to head off to medical school. I started medical school at Texas Tech Health Science Center in Lubbock, Texas. Somehow, I managed to survive and thrive in medical school in spite of violating all the dress codes and known stereotypes of medical students. When I finished medical school, the next step was a pediatric residency in Cleveland, Ohio, where I thought I was going to freeze to death, but I did learn a ton about pediatrics.,

In July of 2000 I started practicing pediatrics in Oak Ridge, Tennessee, where I have been ever since.